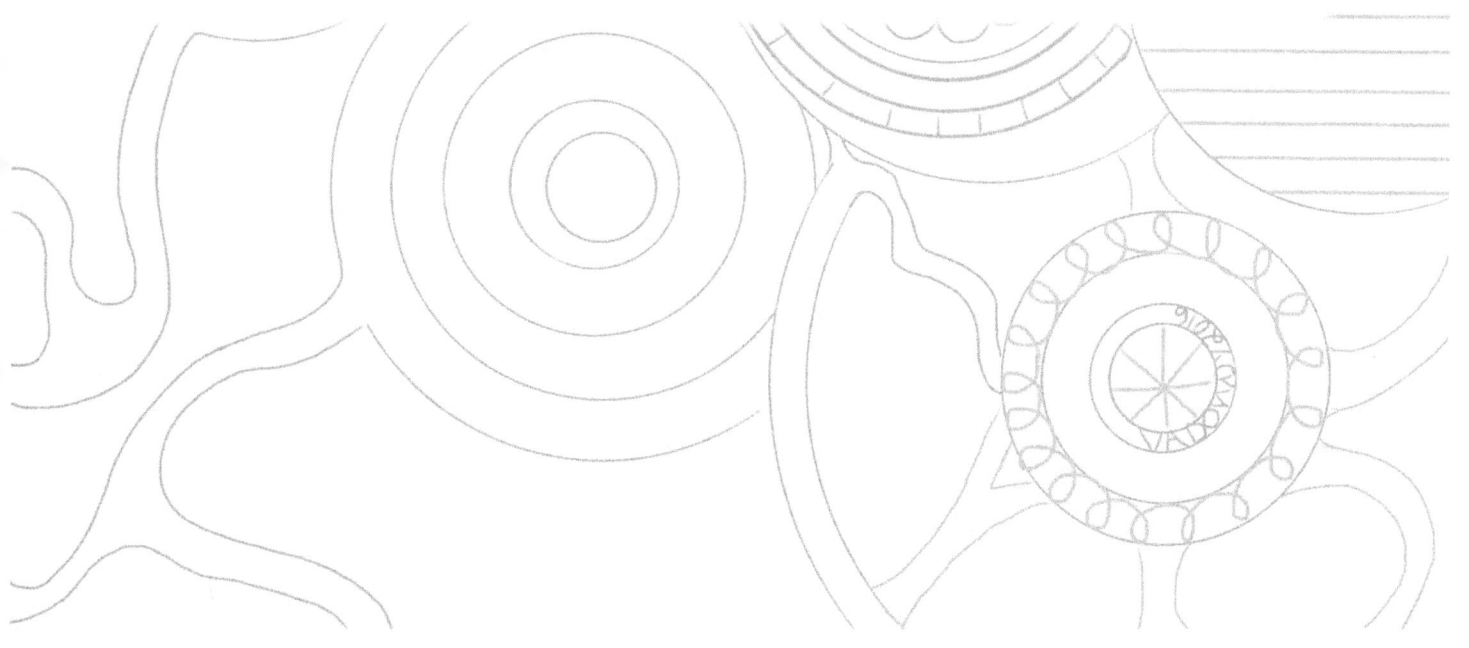

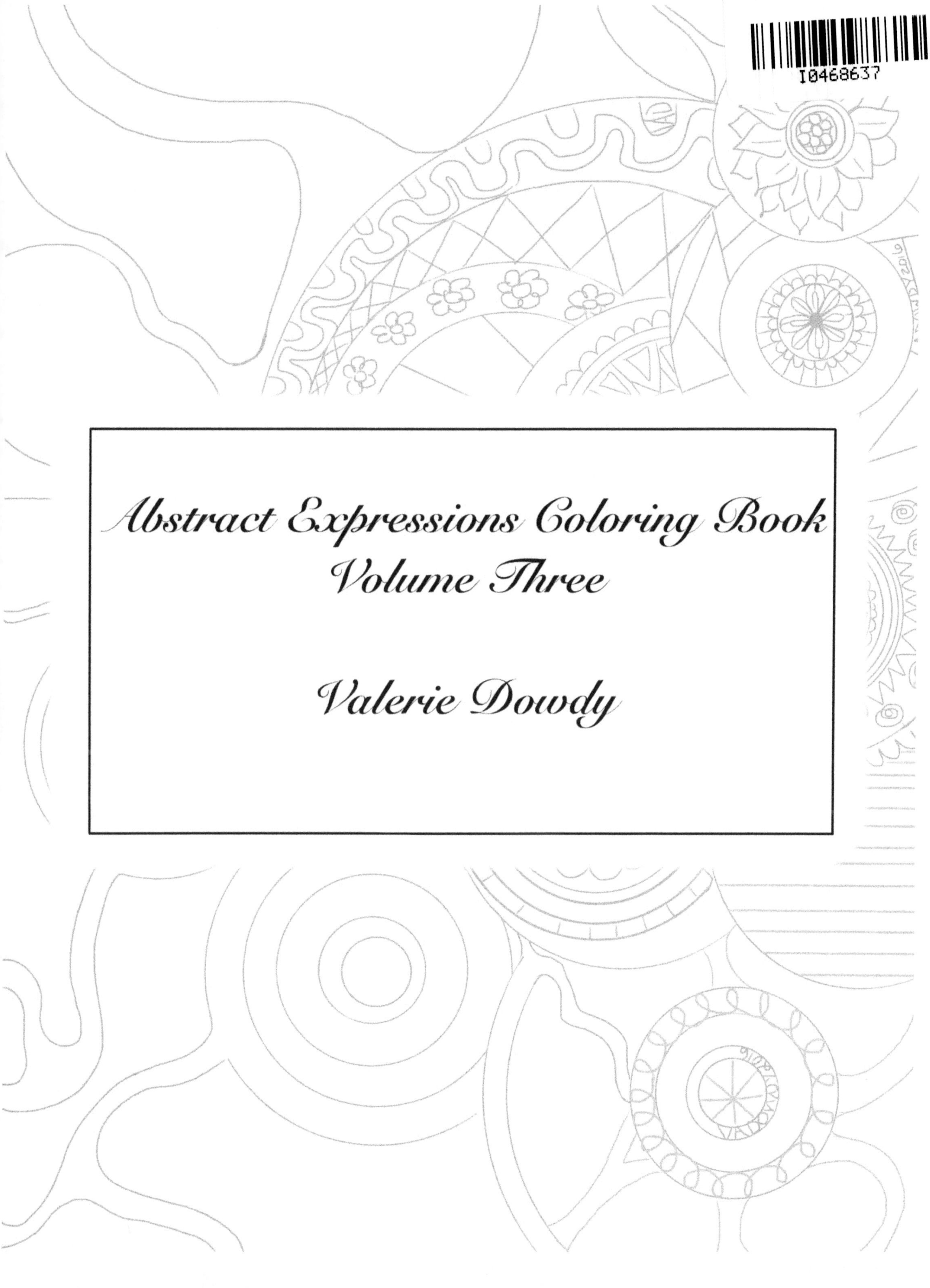

Abstract Expressions Coloring Book
Volume Three

Valerie Dowdy

SBN-10: 978-1523787029
ISBN-13: 1523787023

This one is dedicated to my husband for always convincing me I can...
Remember: Life is about using the whole box of crayons
-Rupaul-

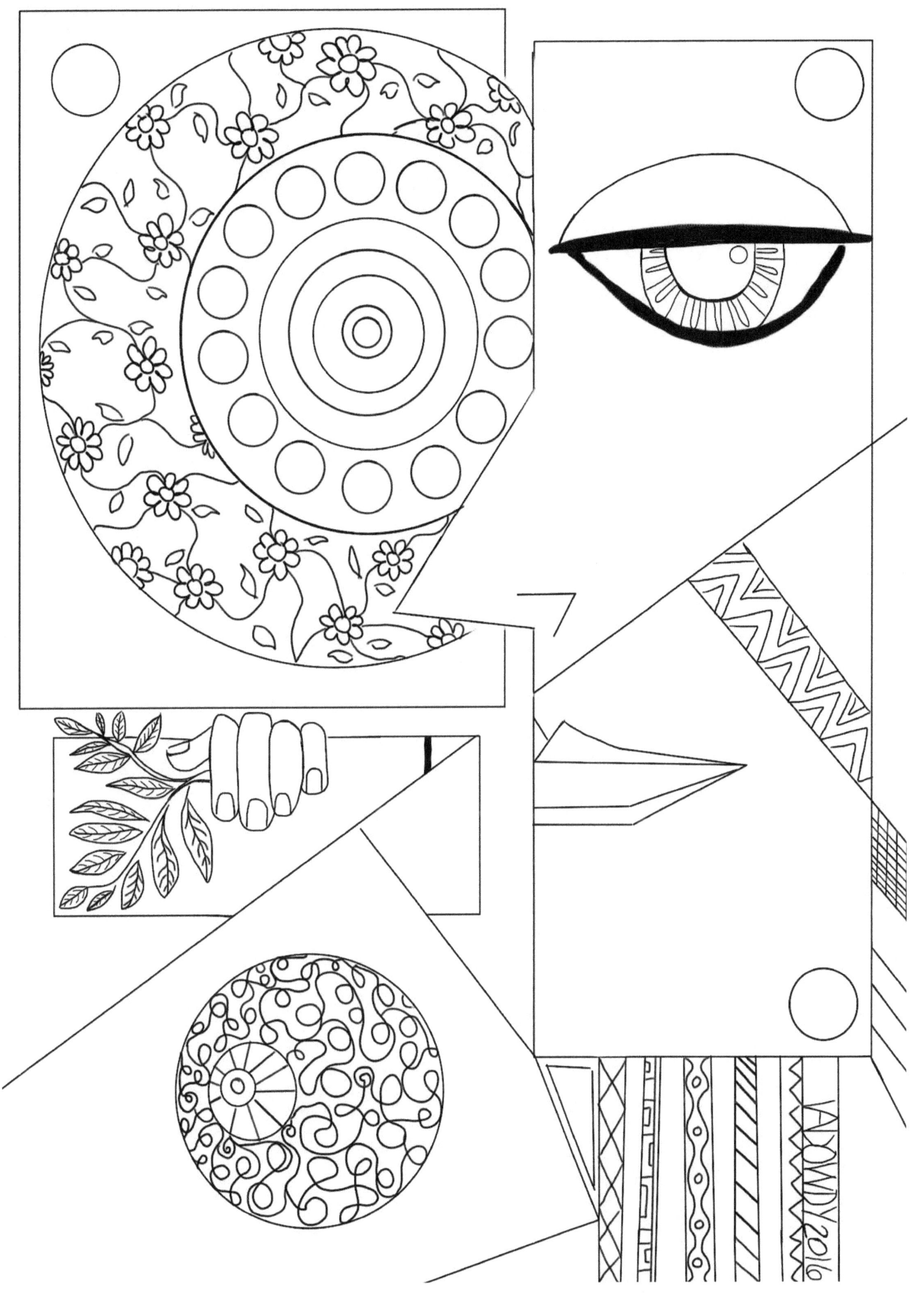

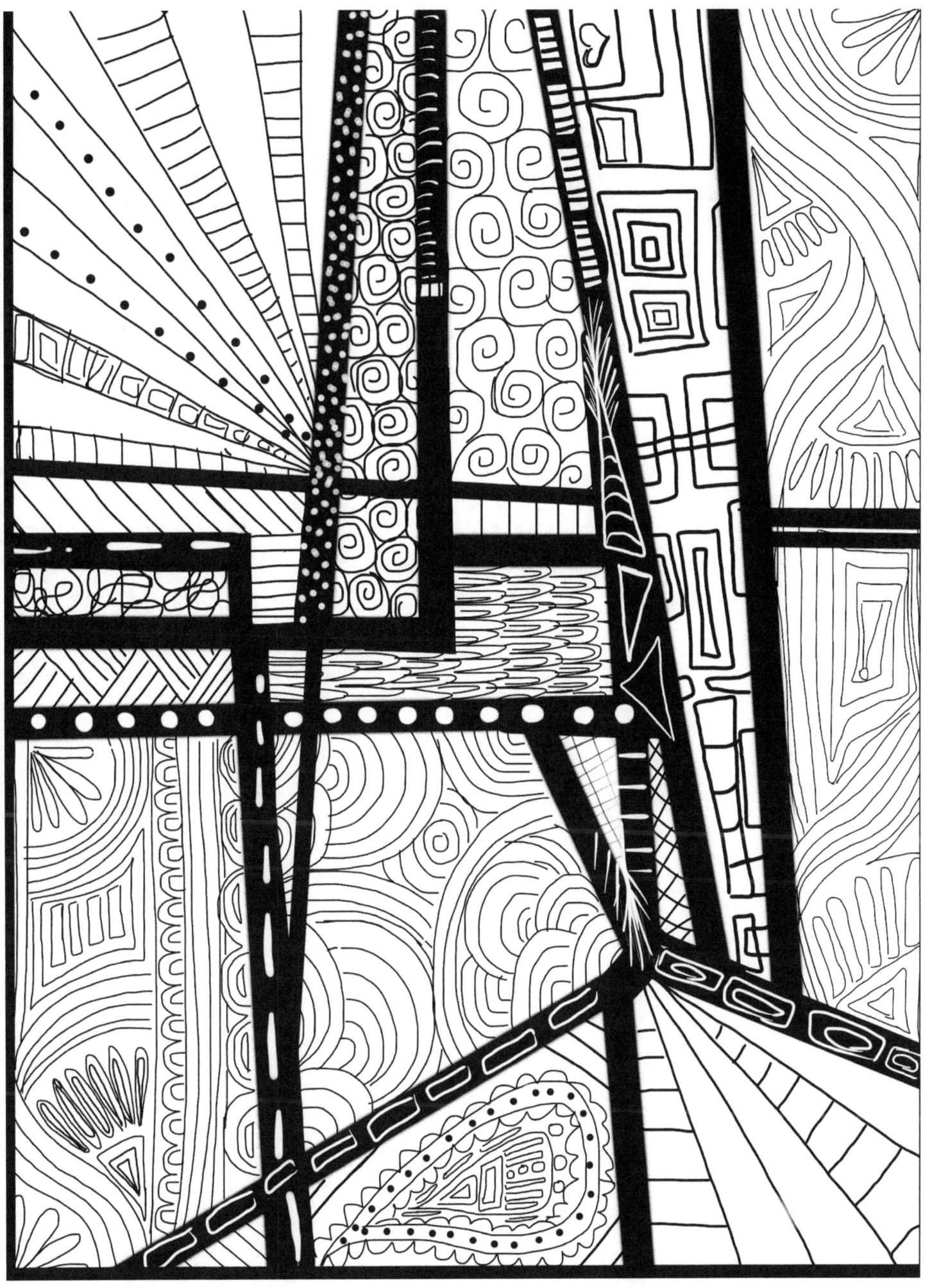

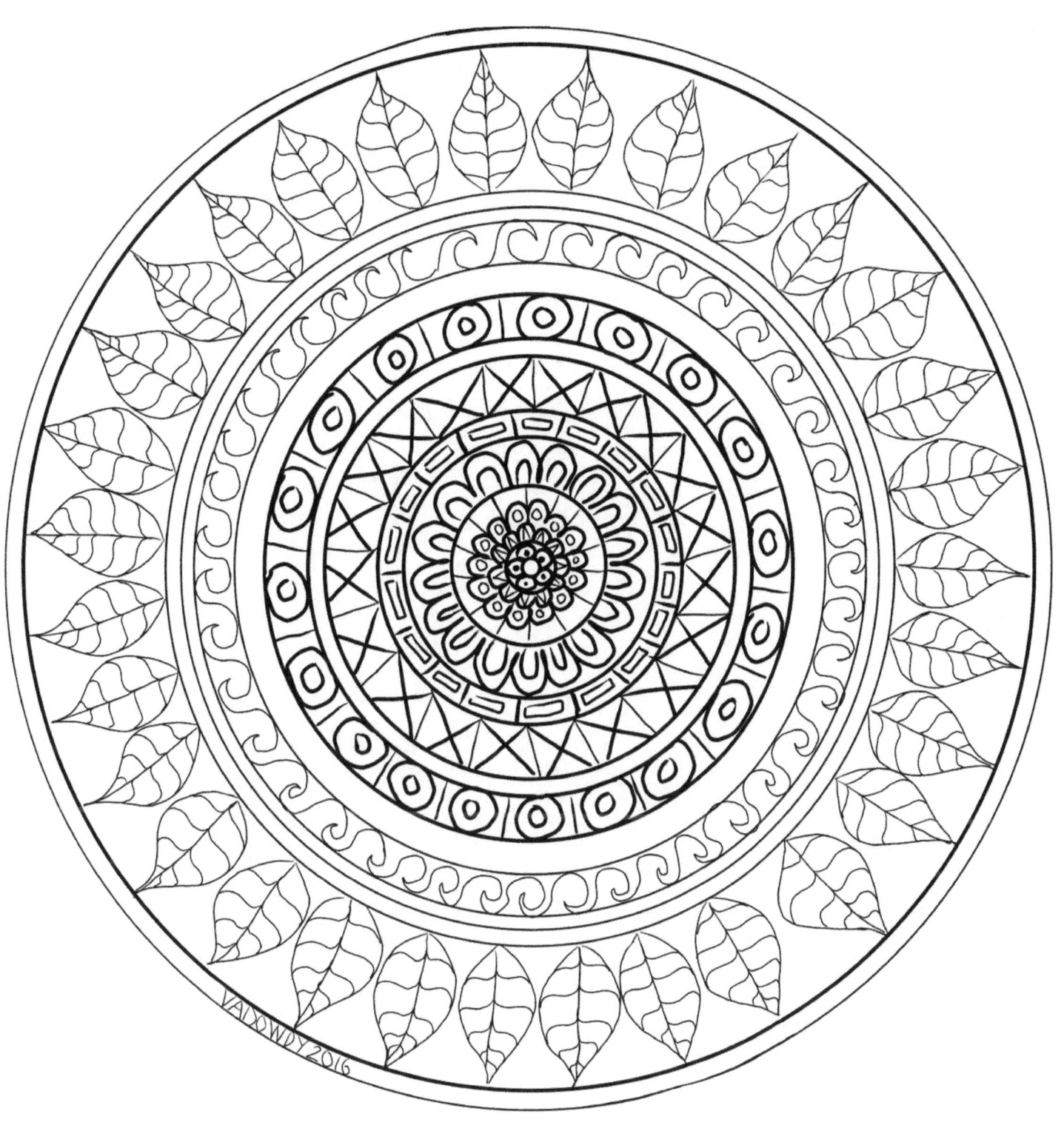

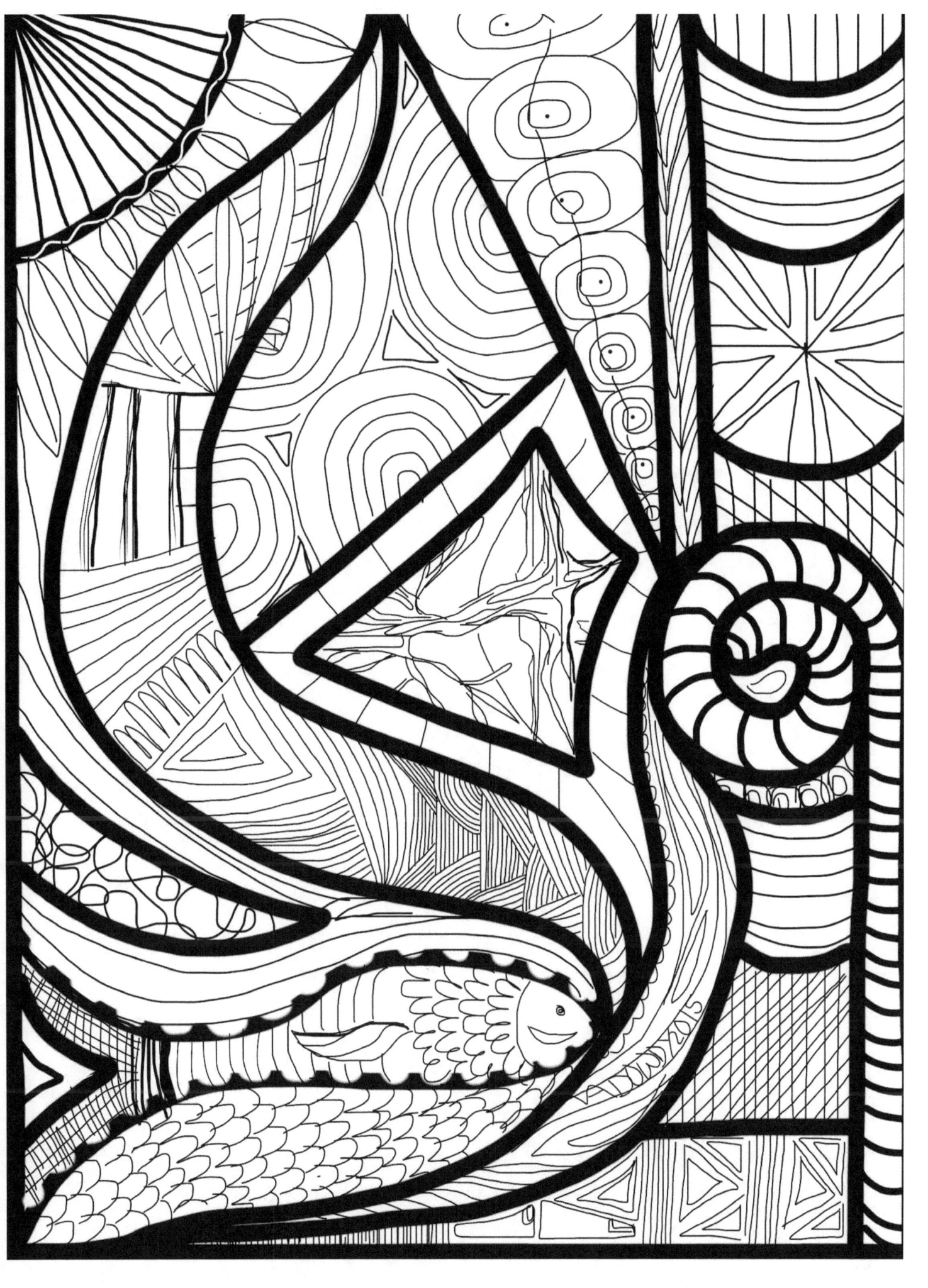

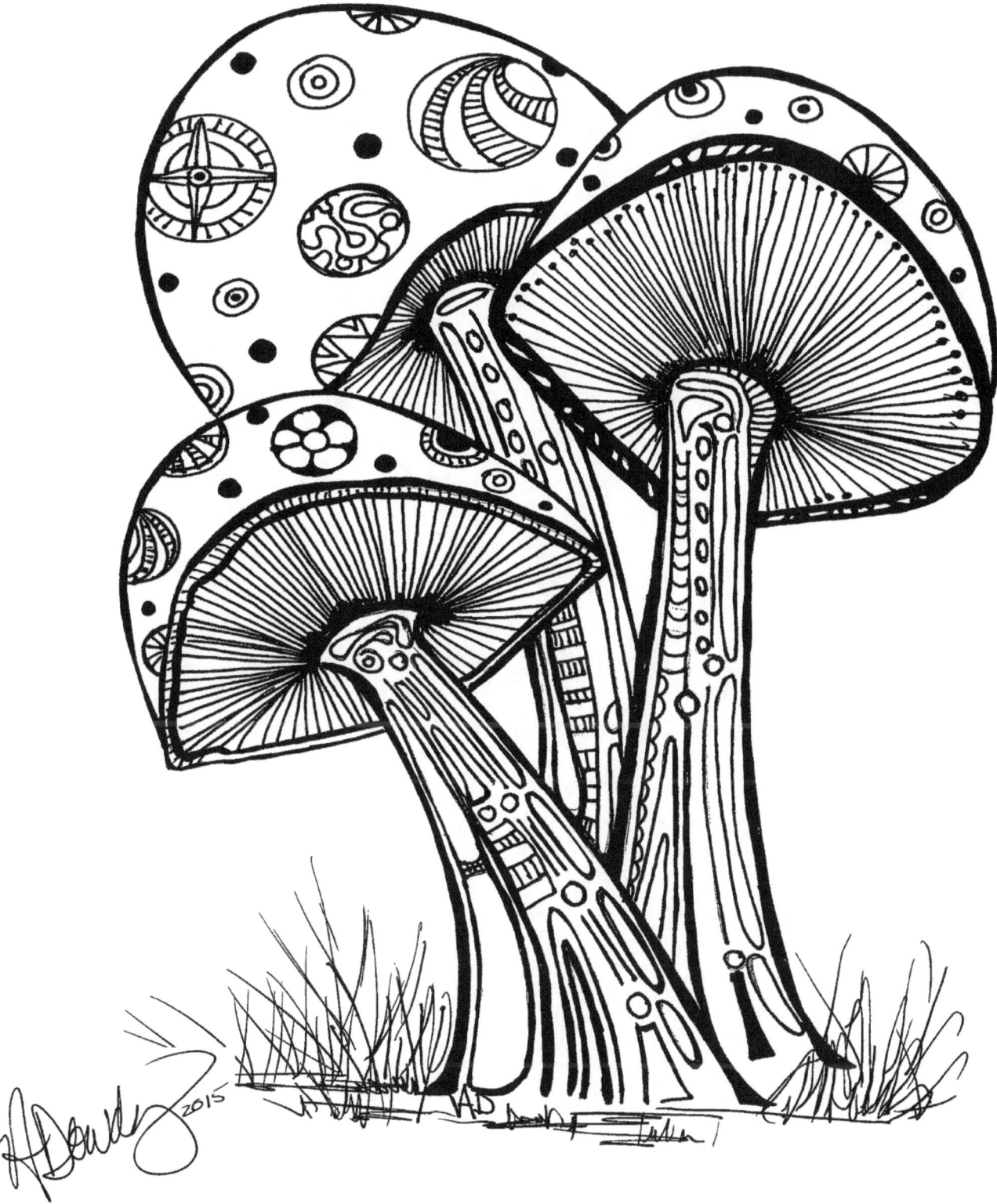

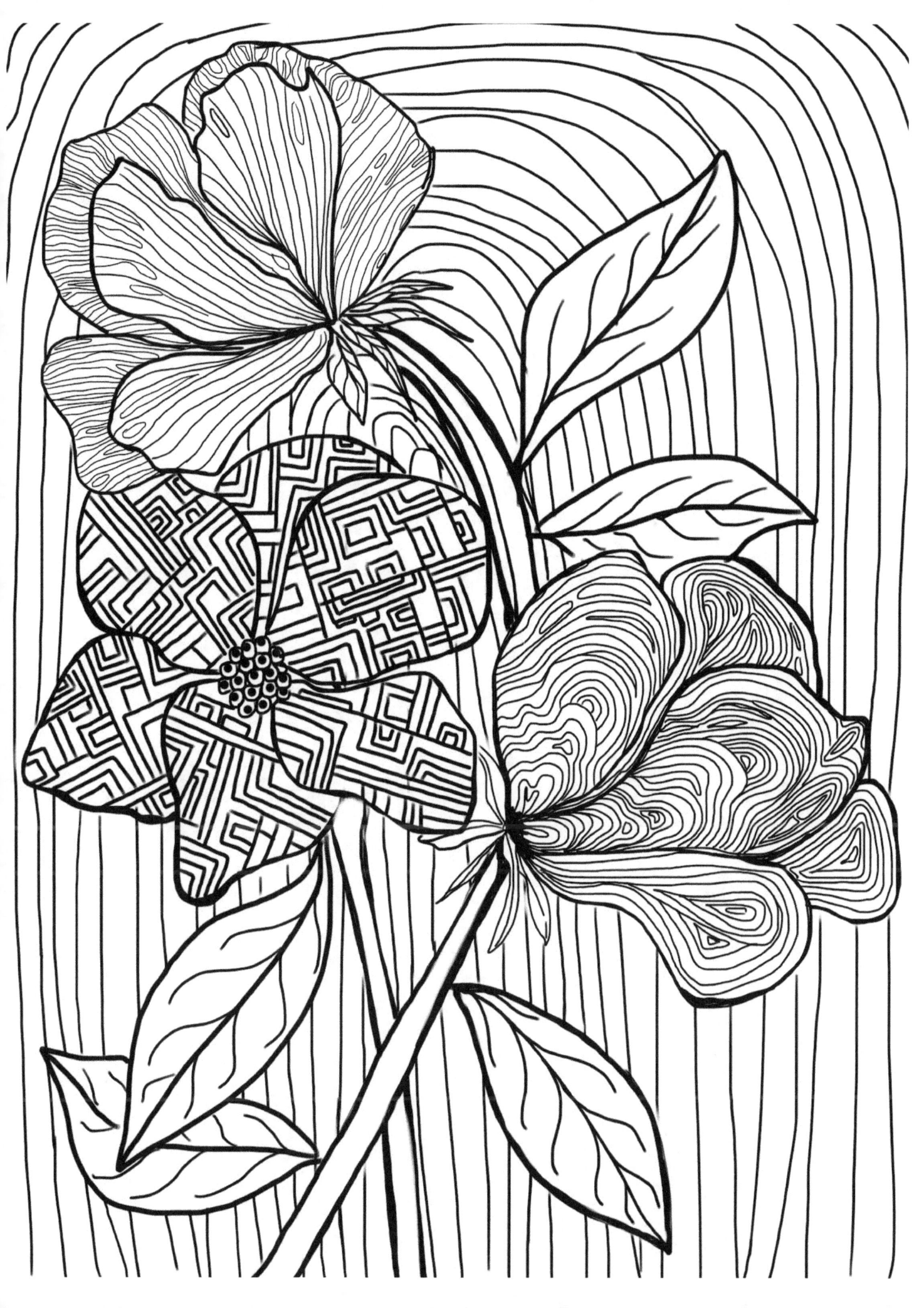

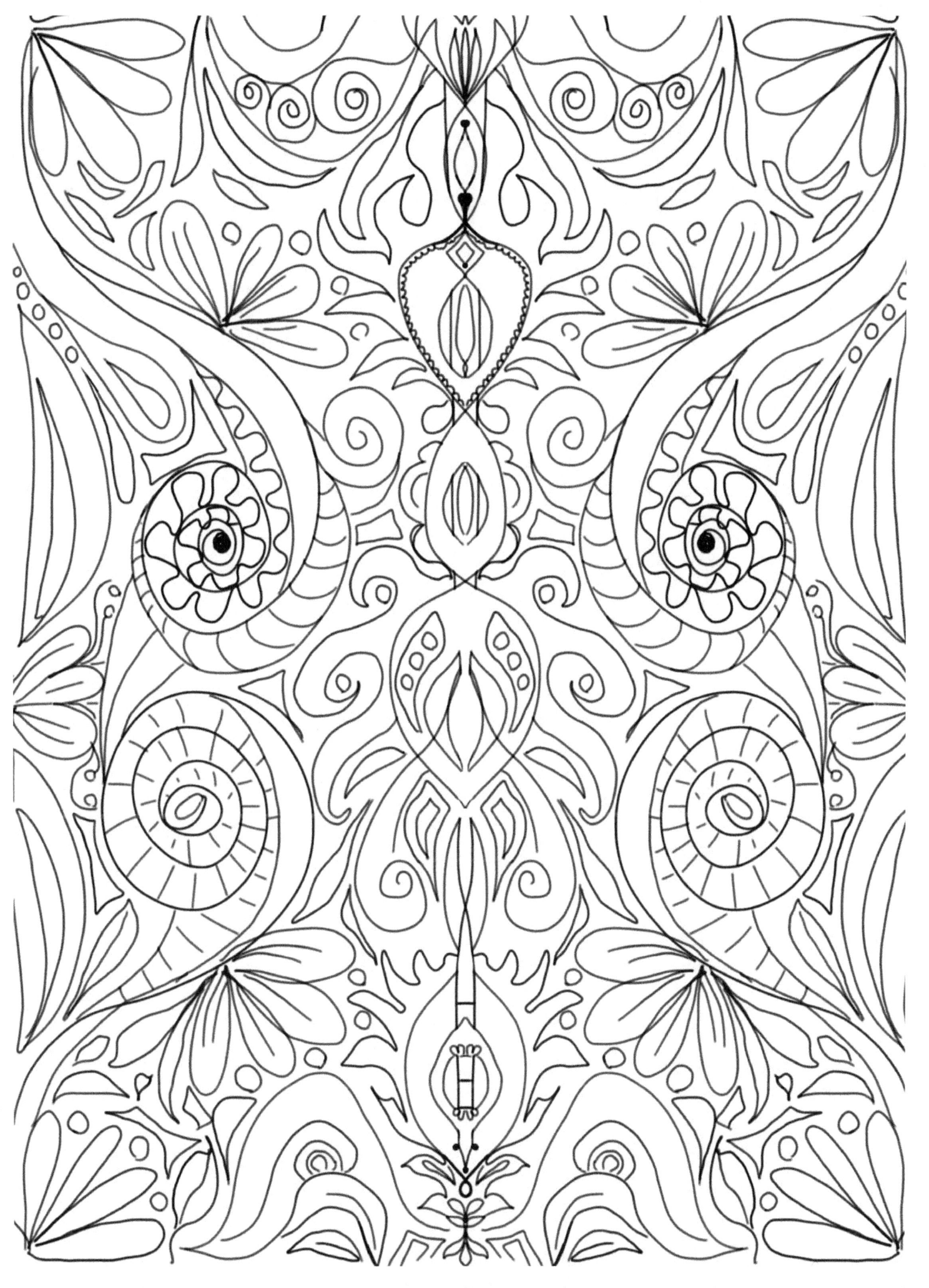

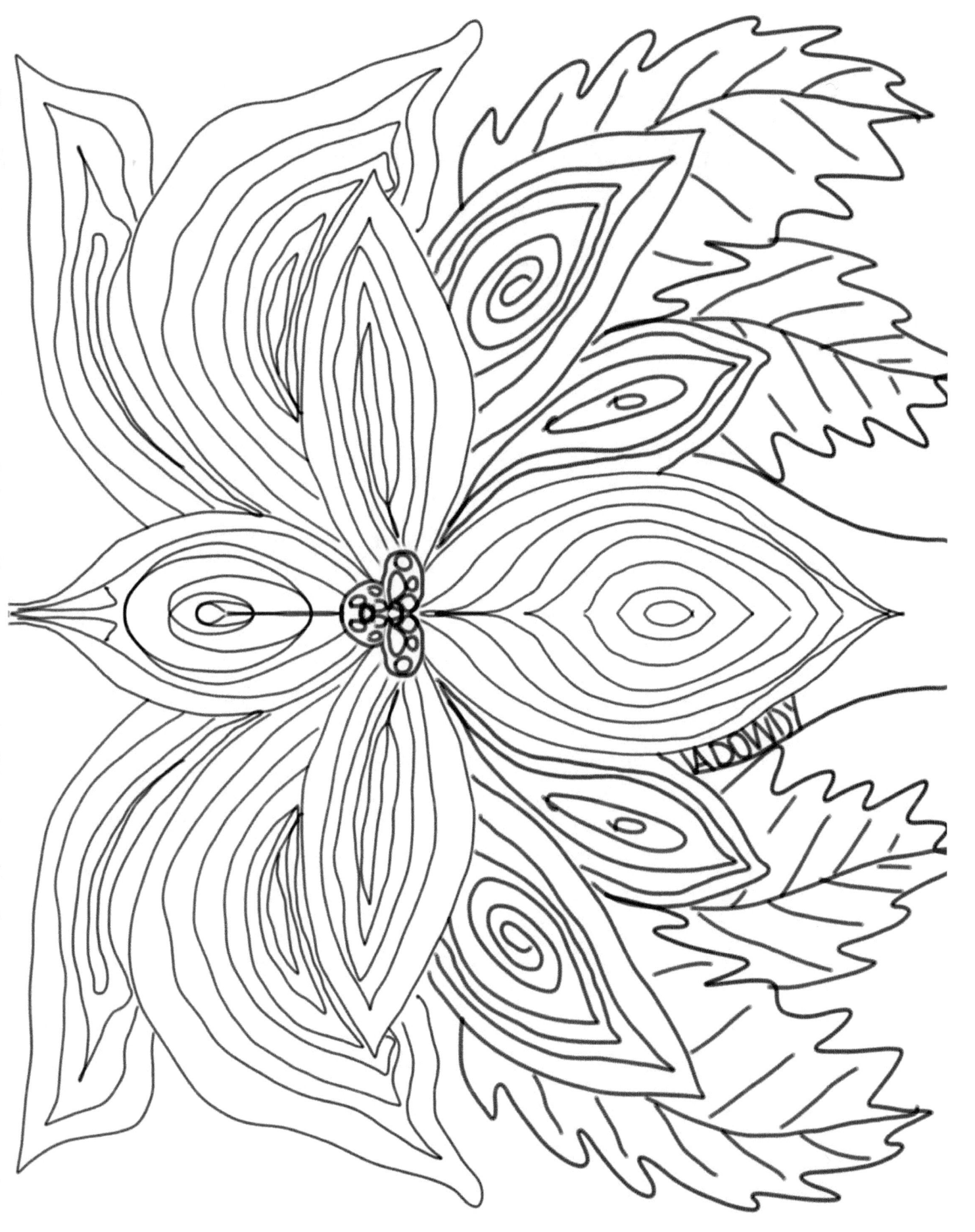

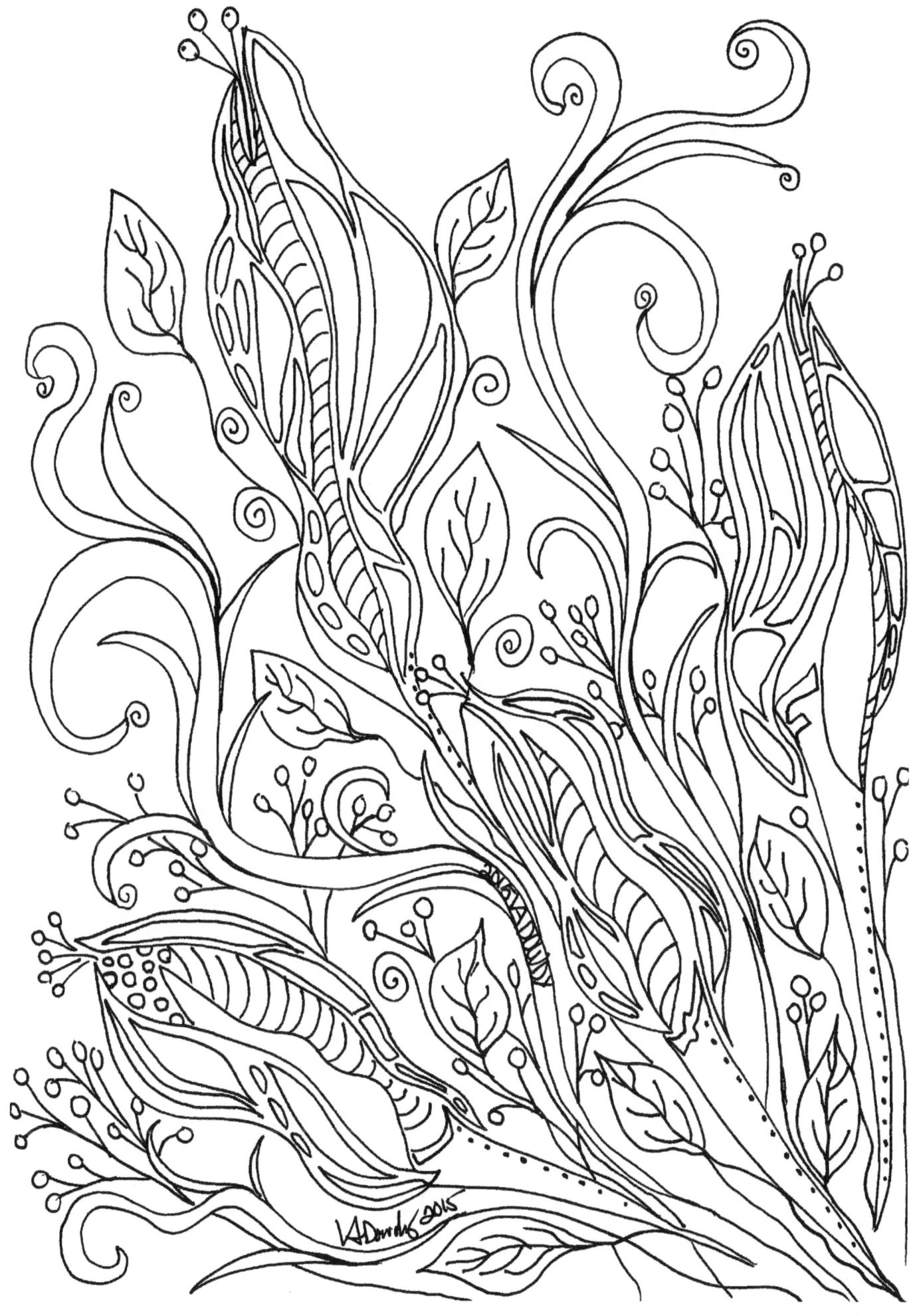

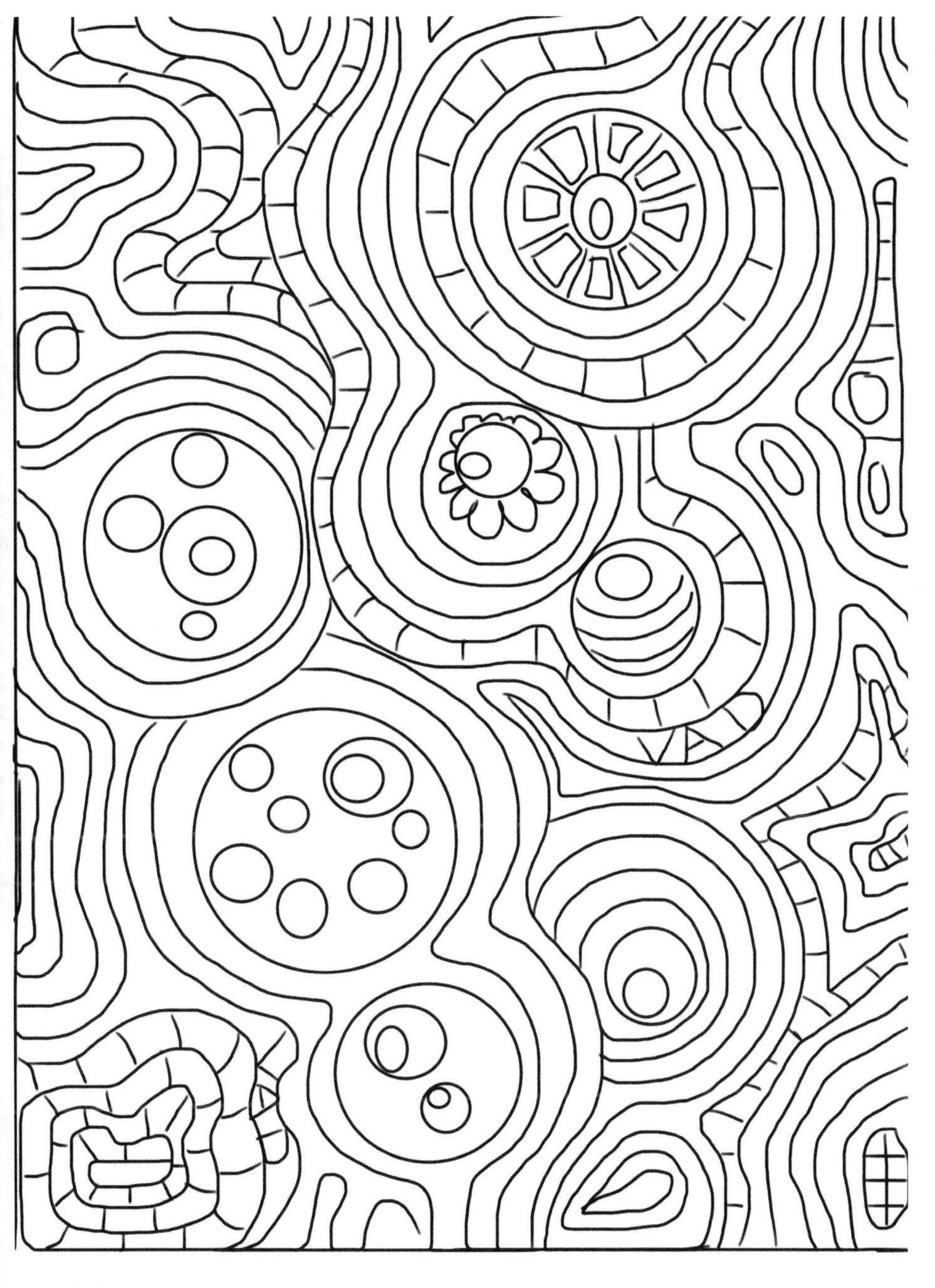

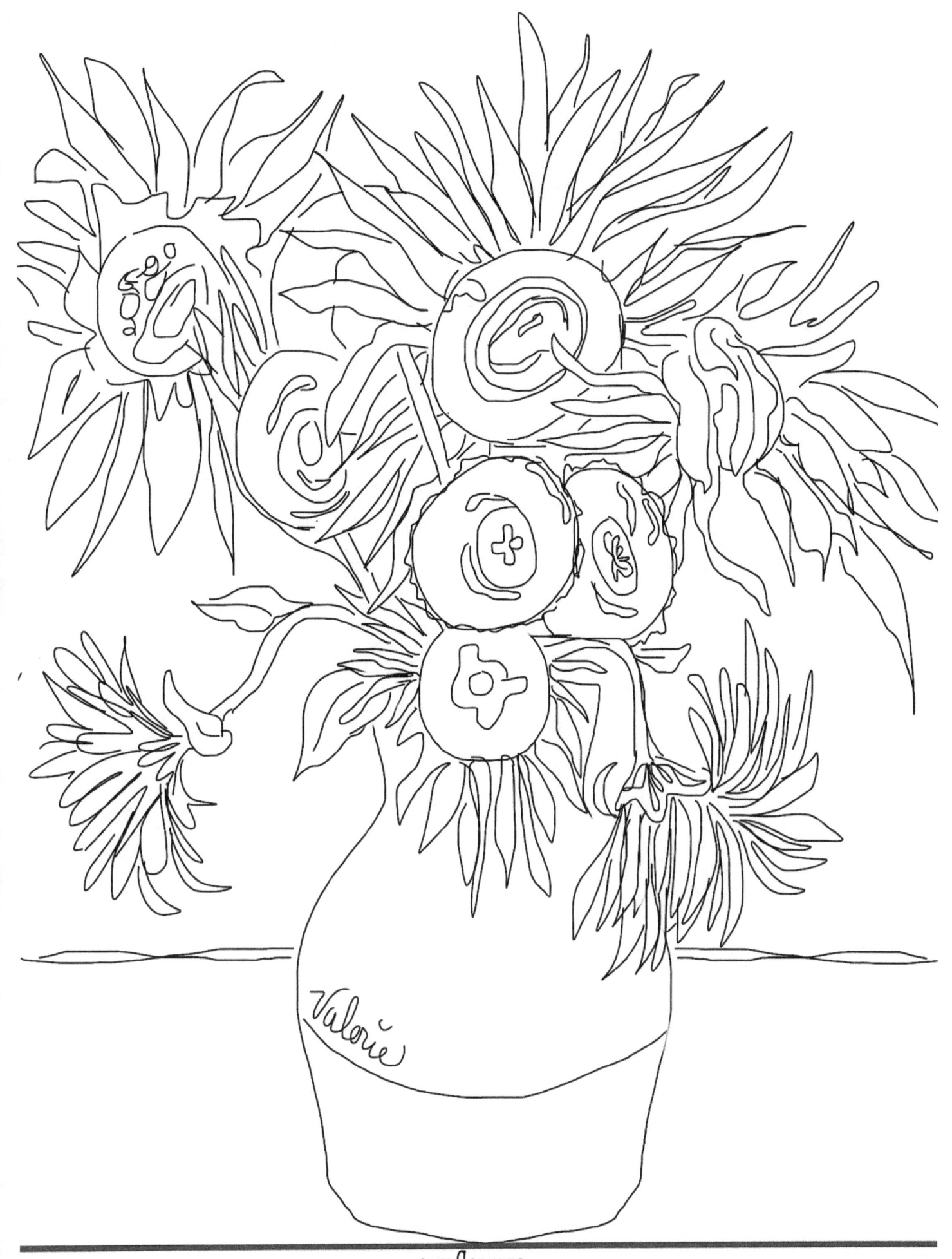

sunflowers

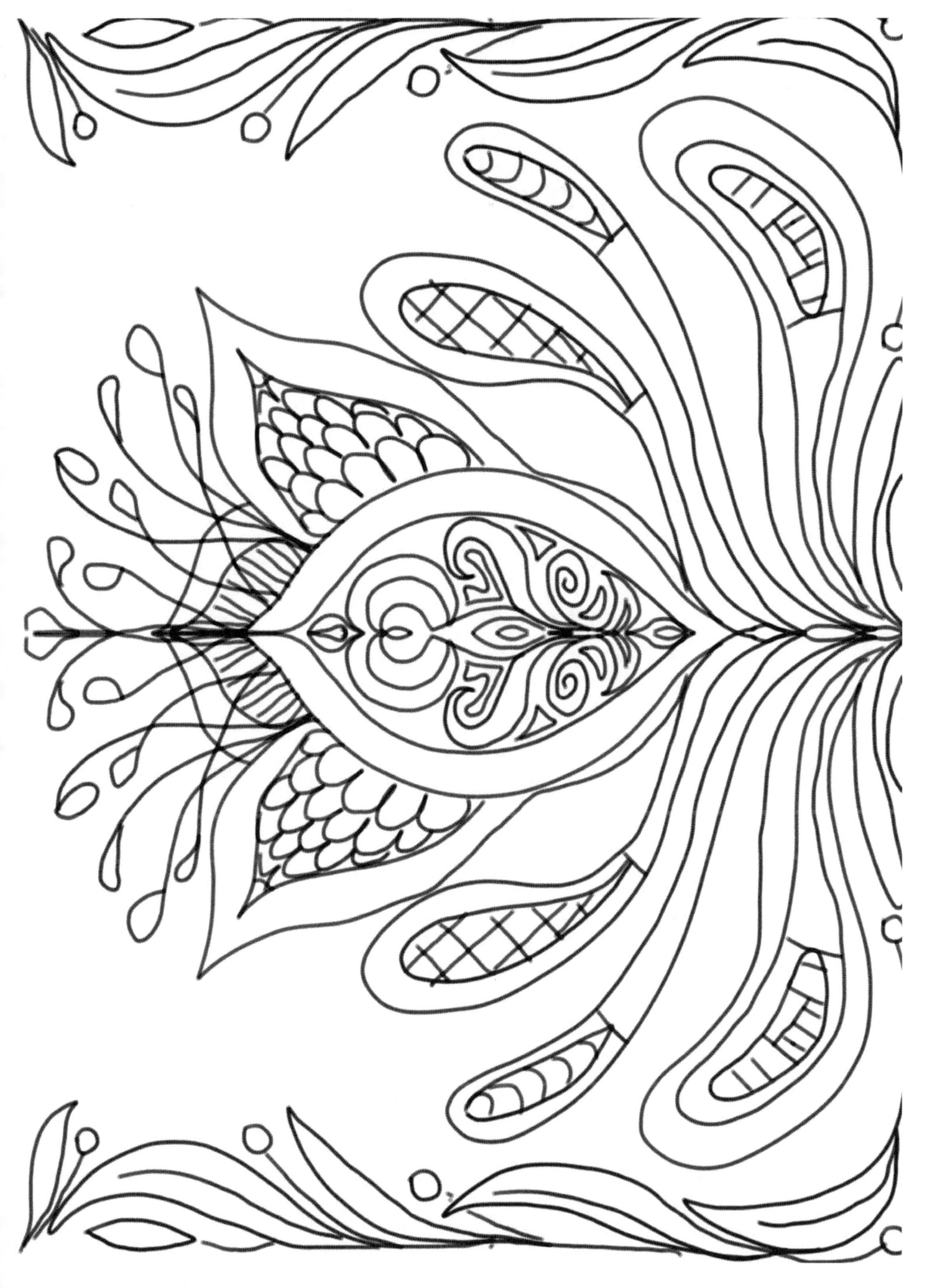

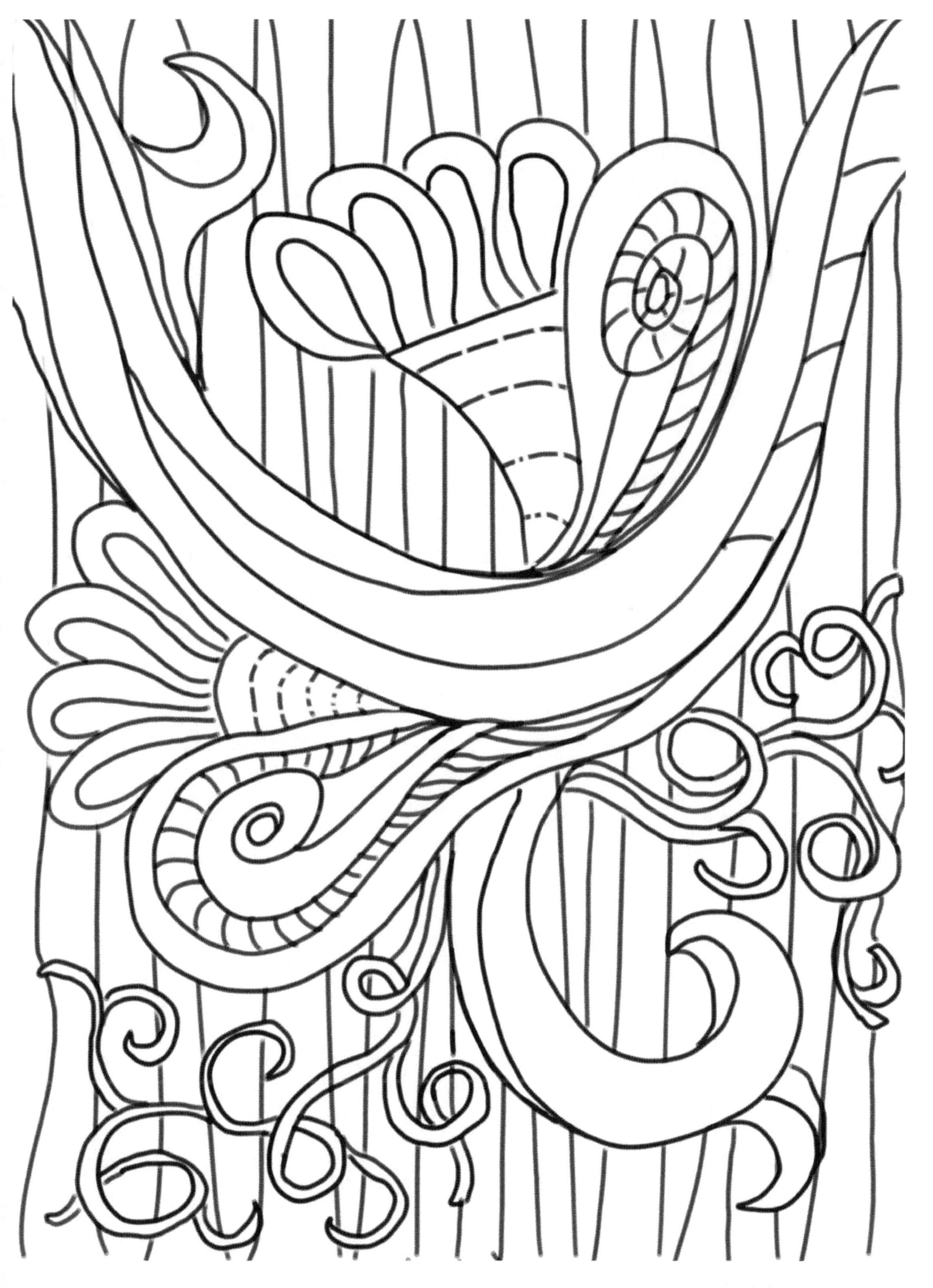

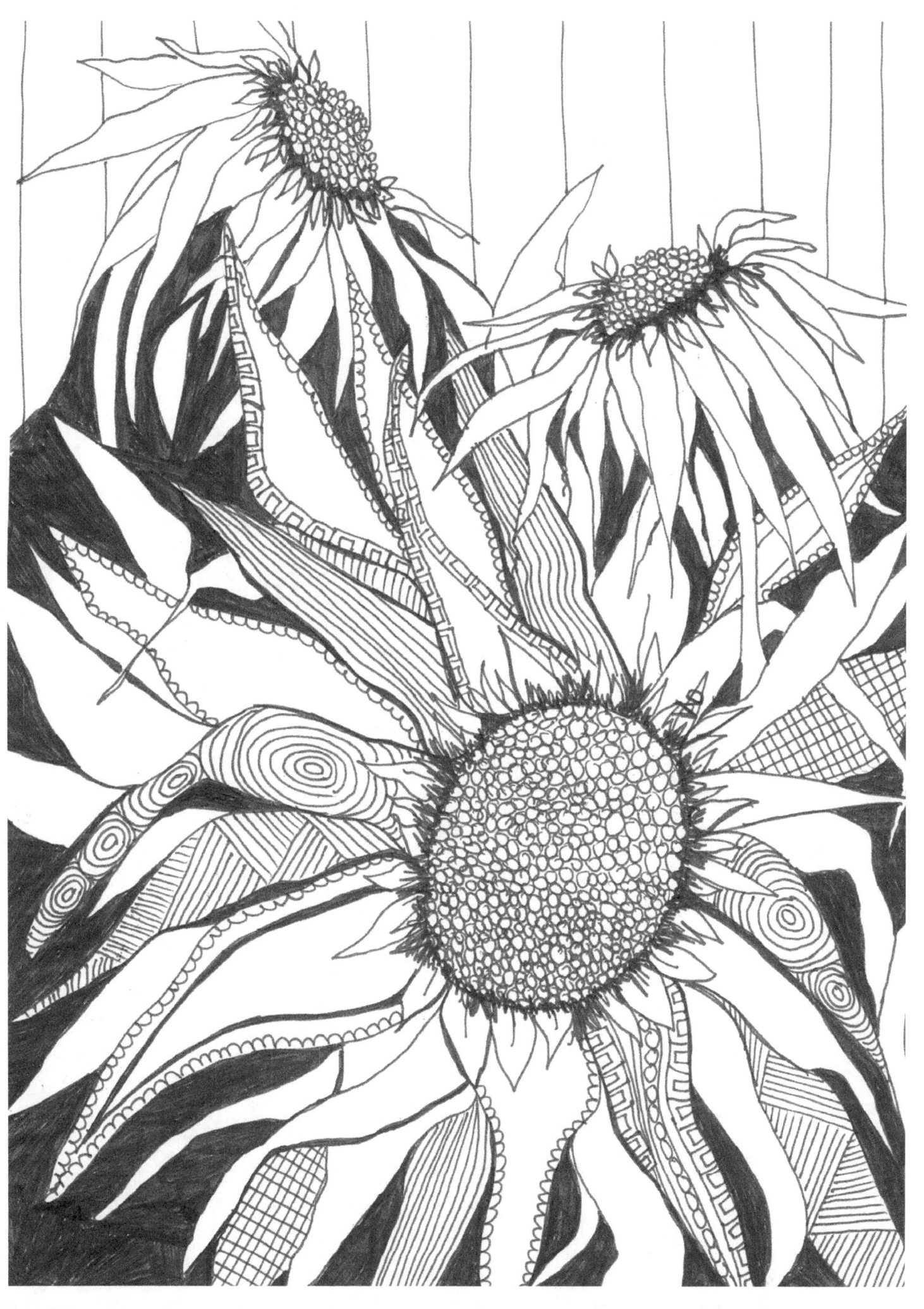

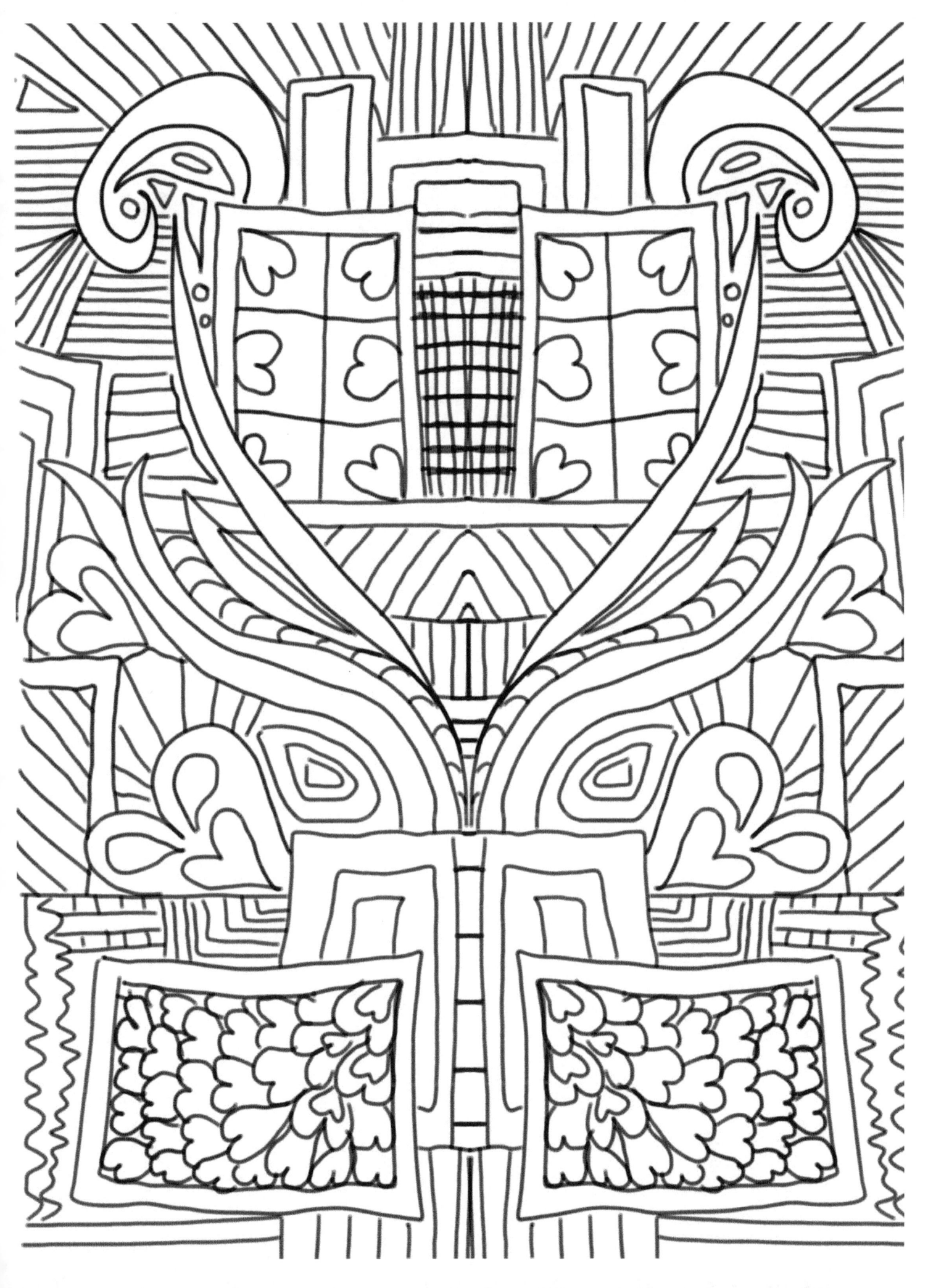

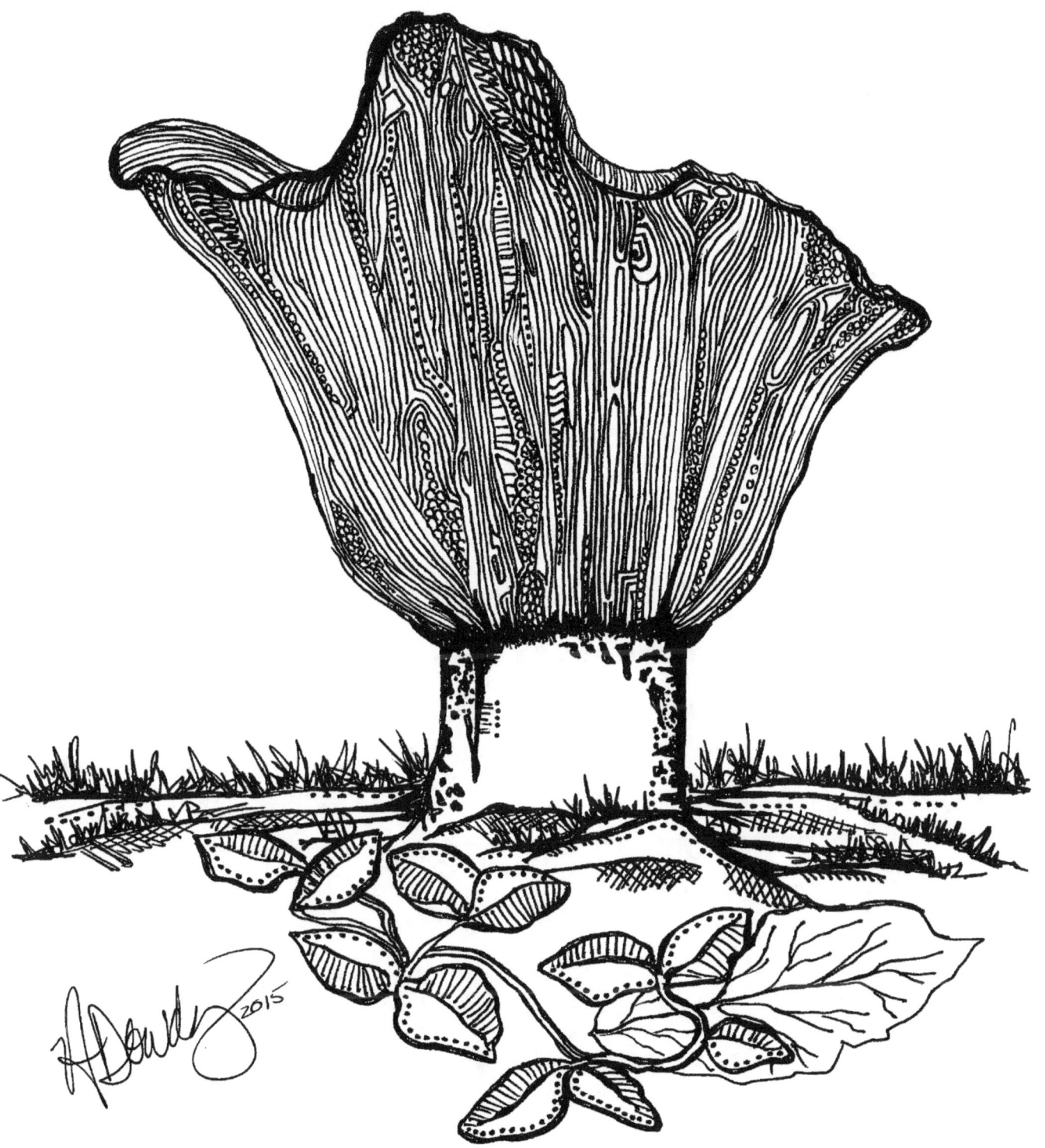

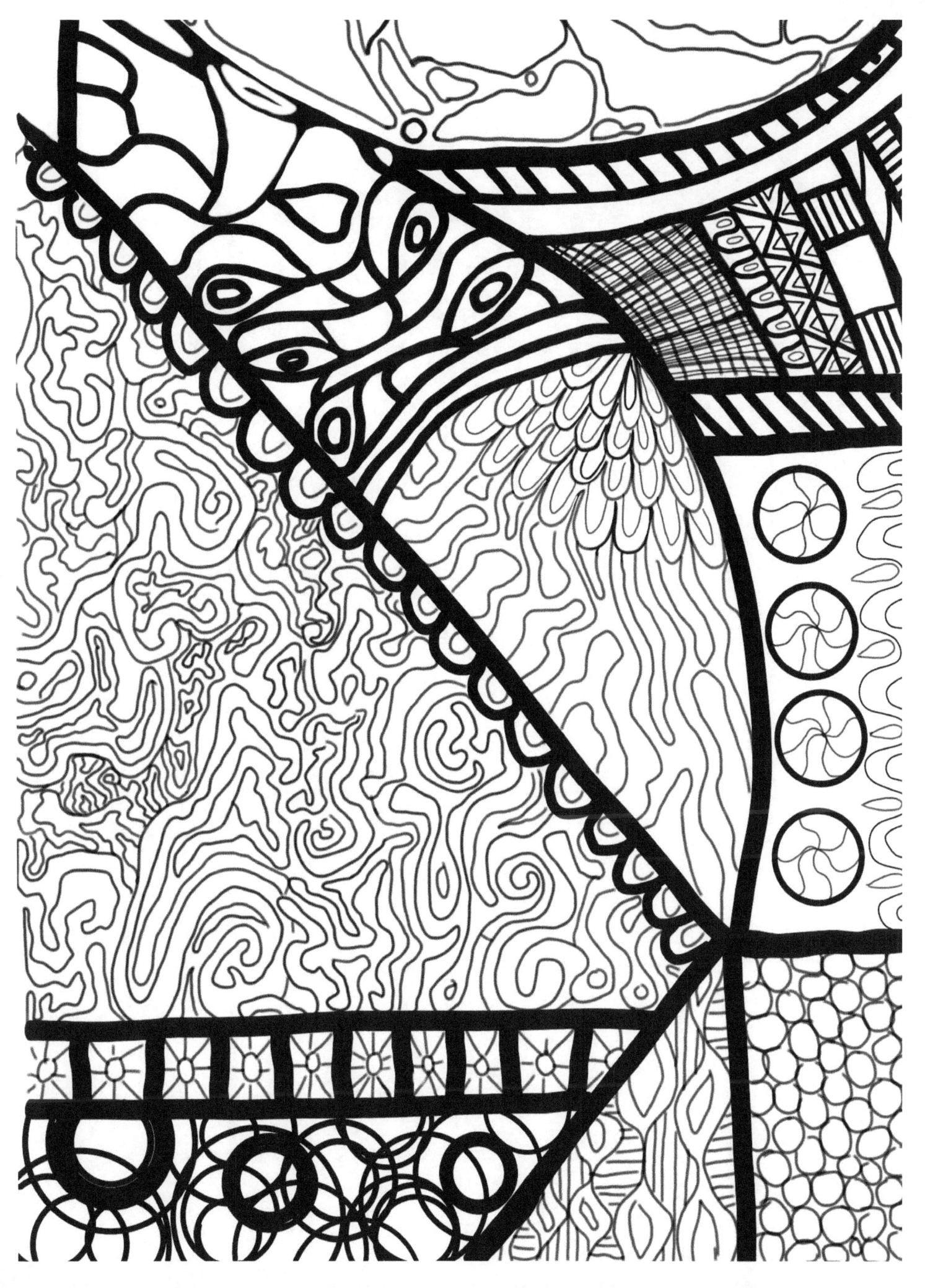

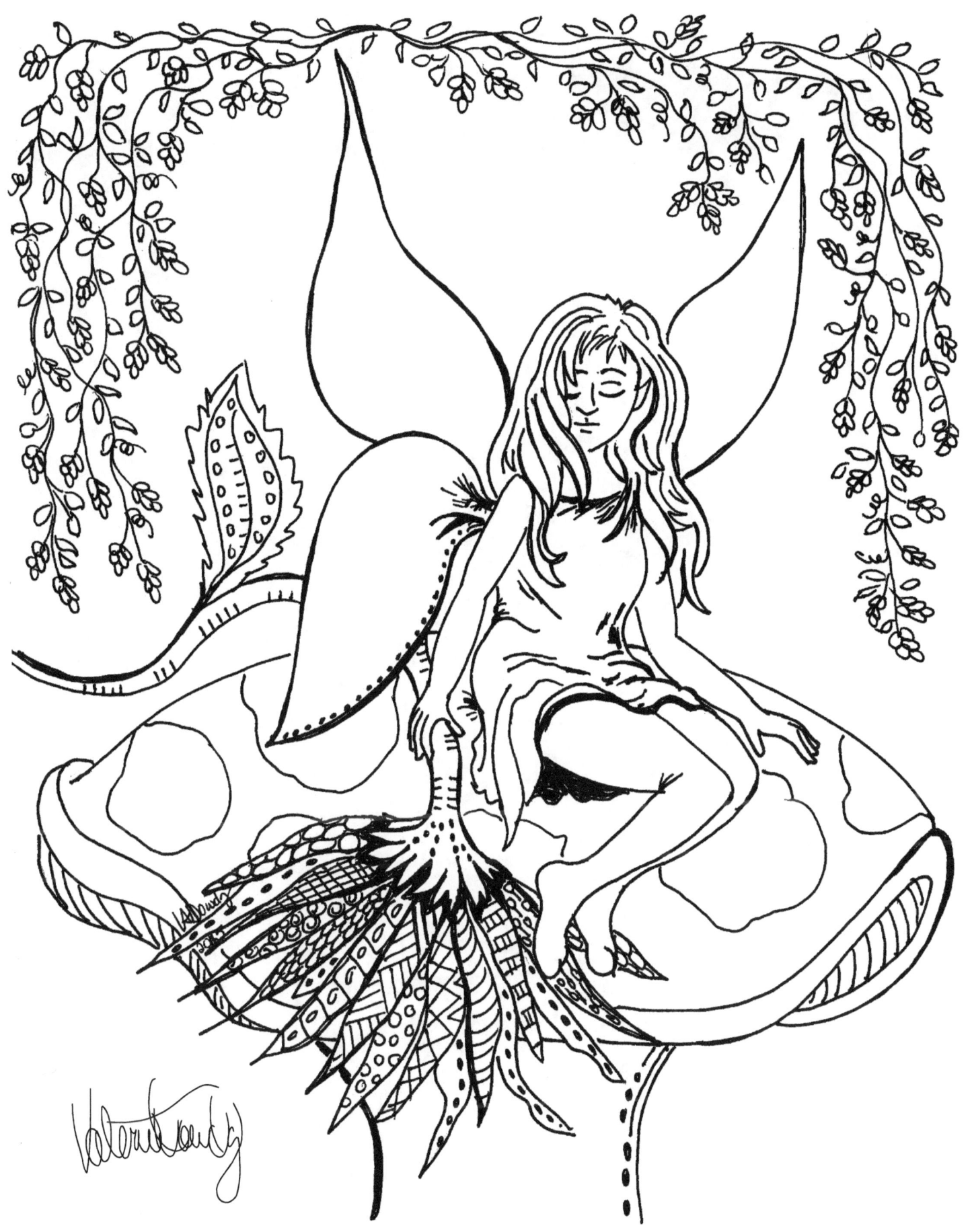

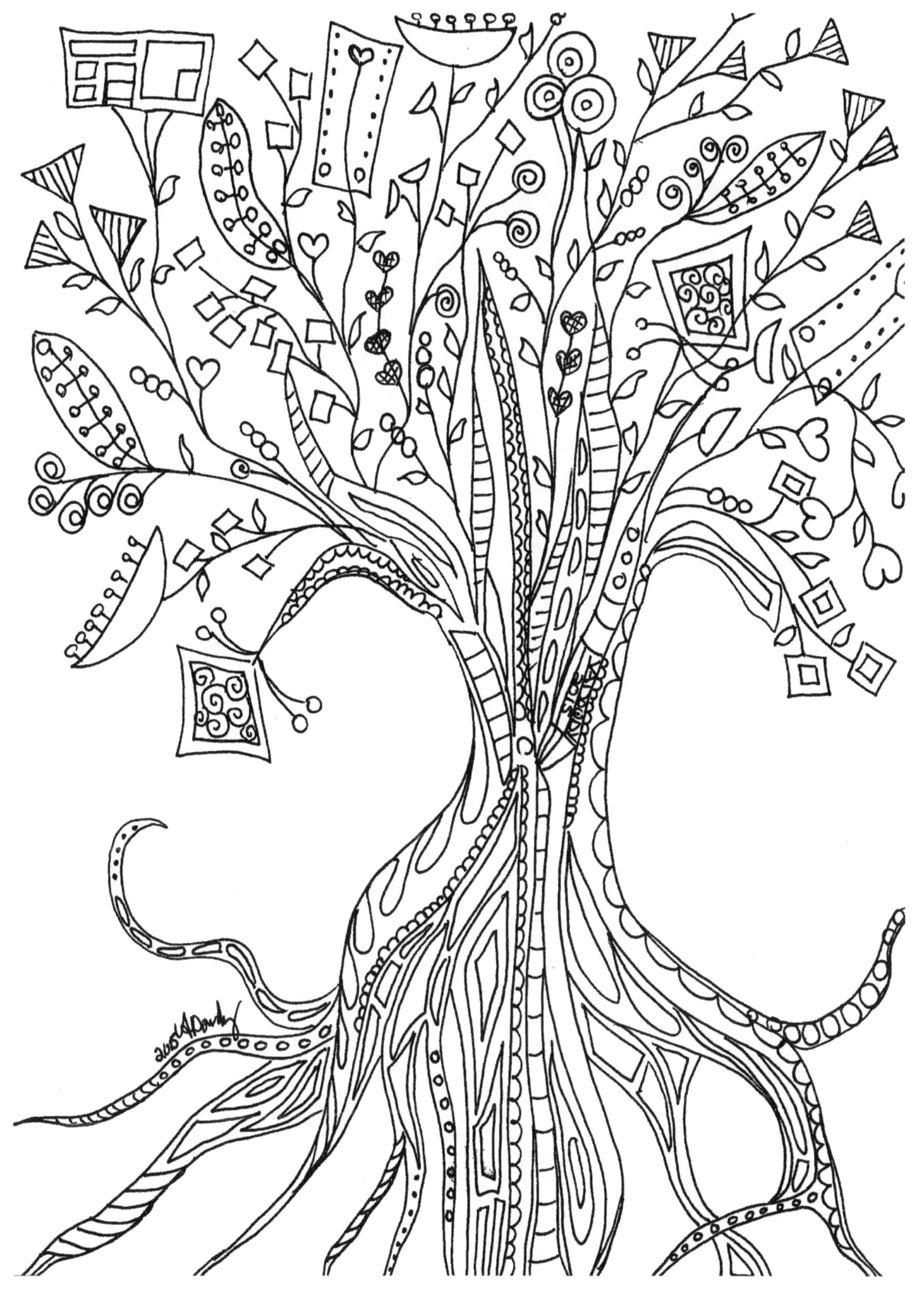

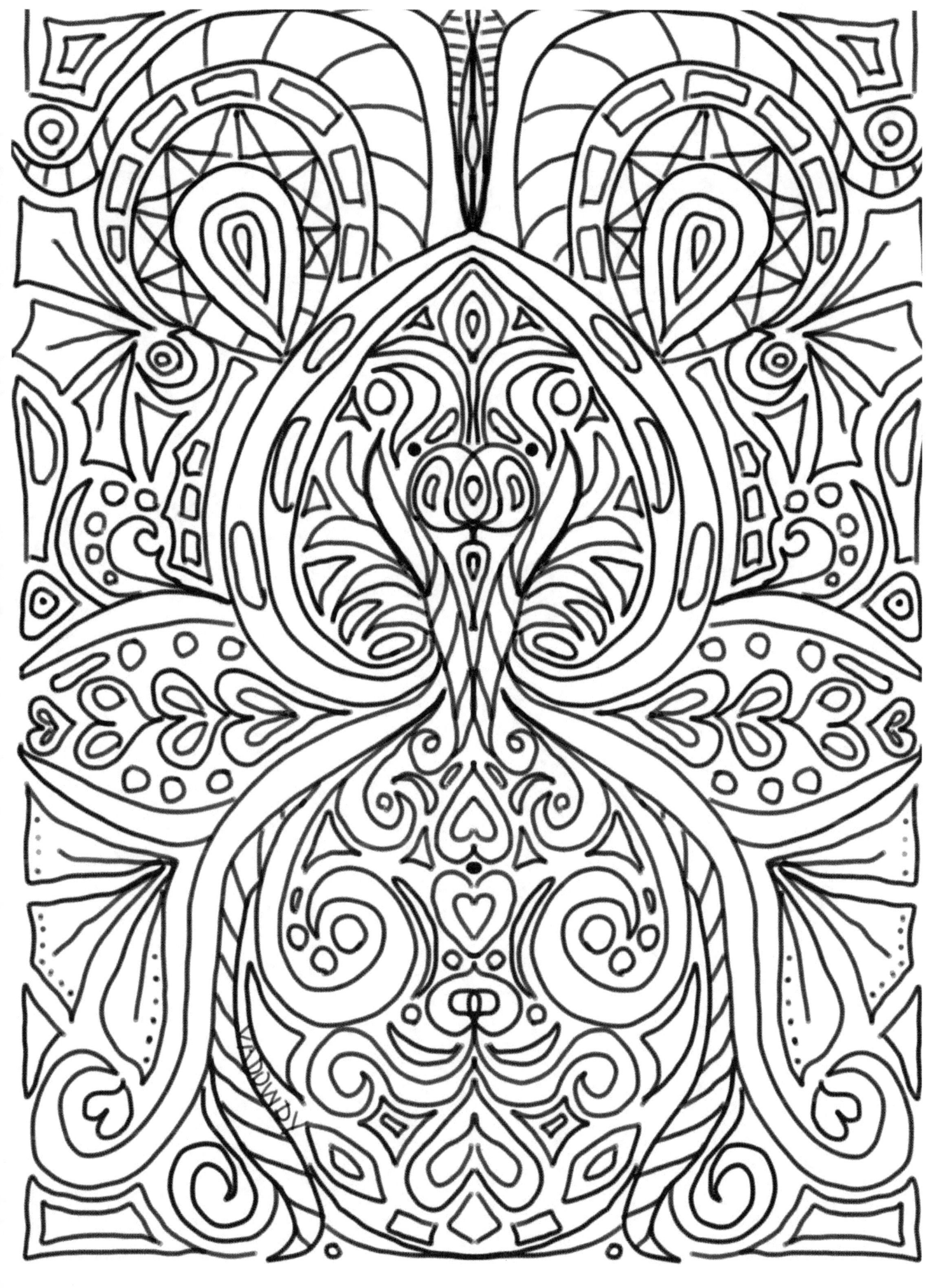

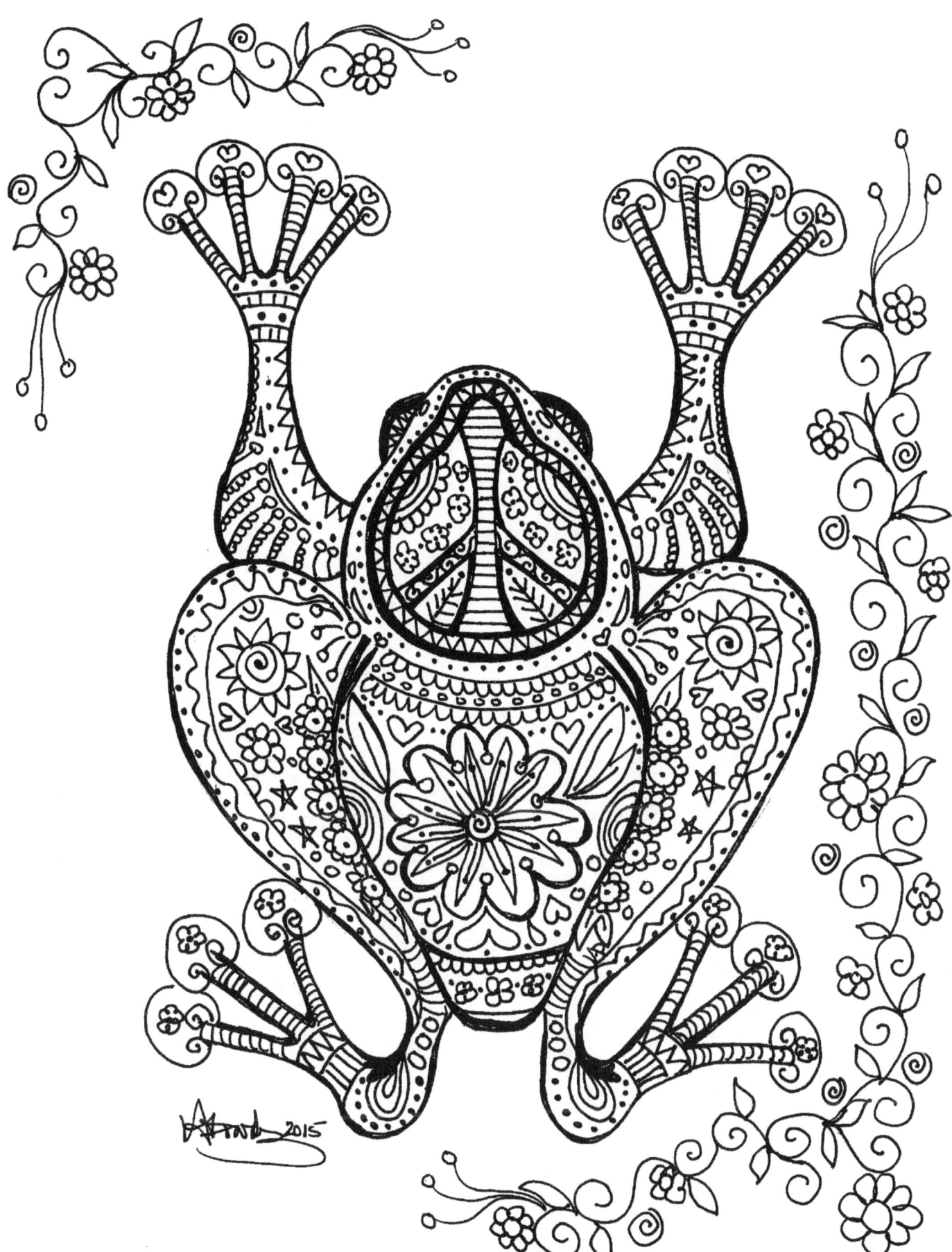

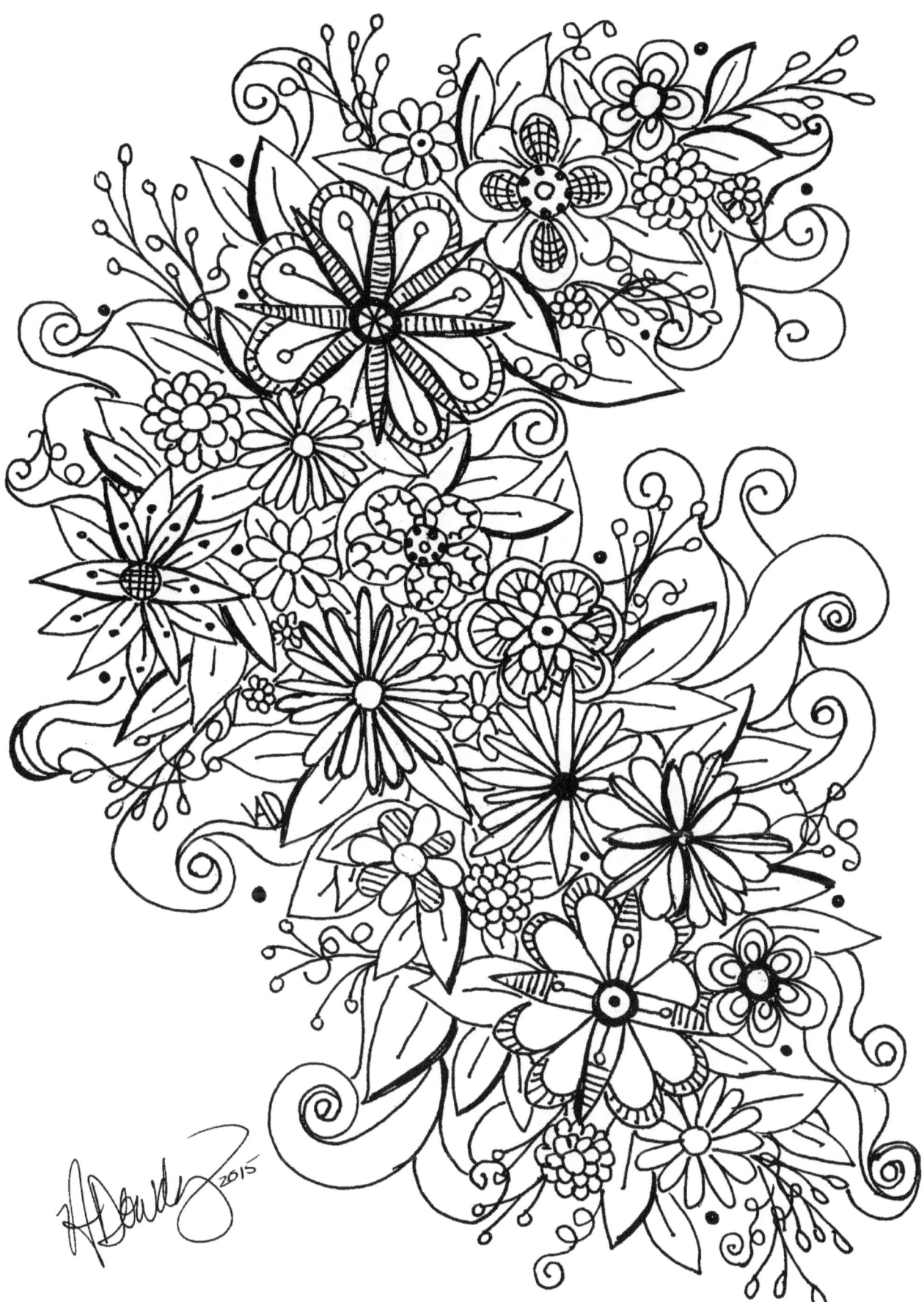

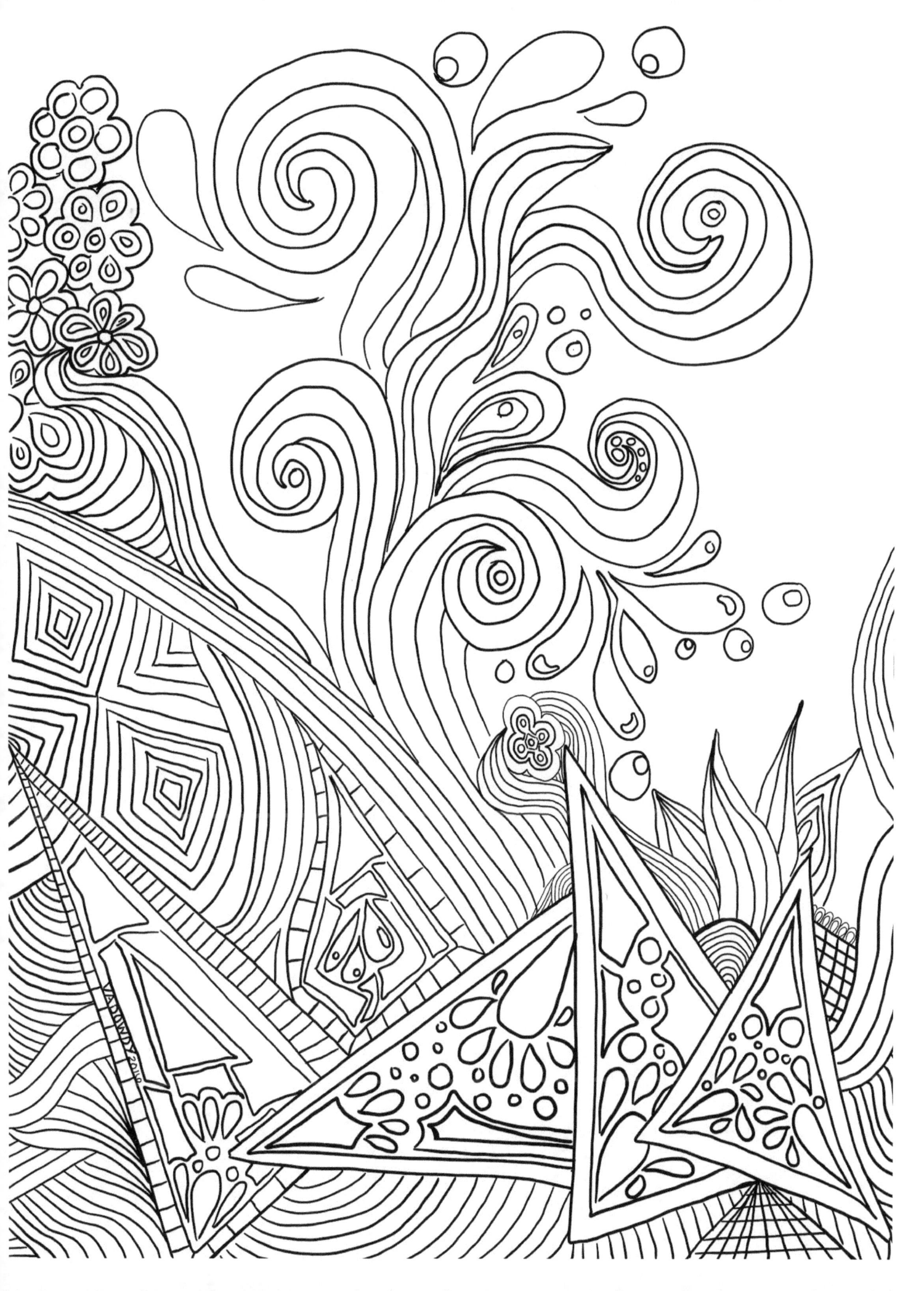

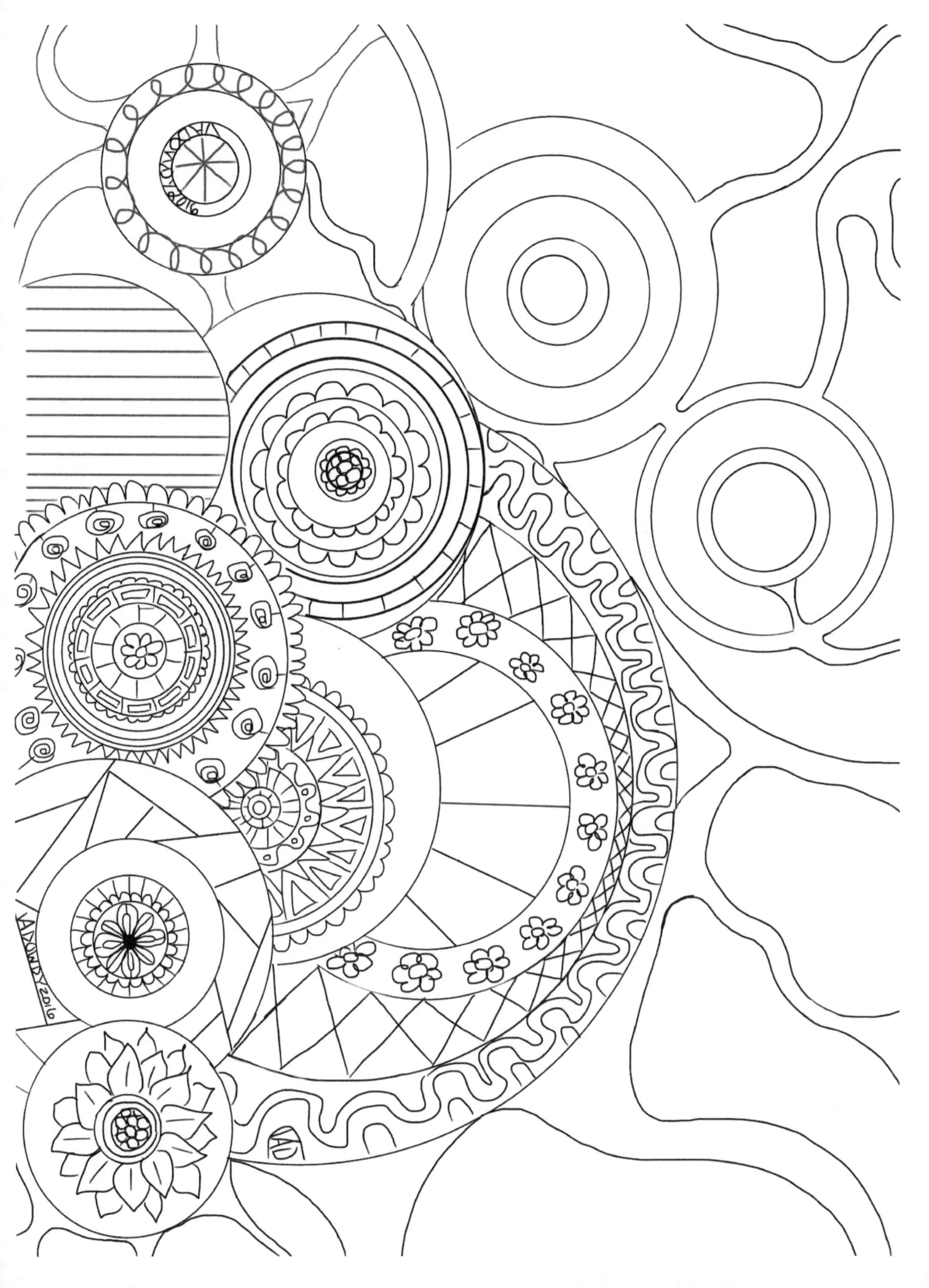

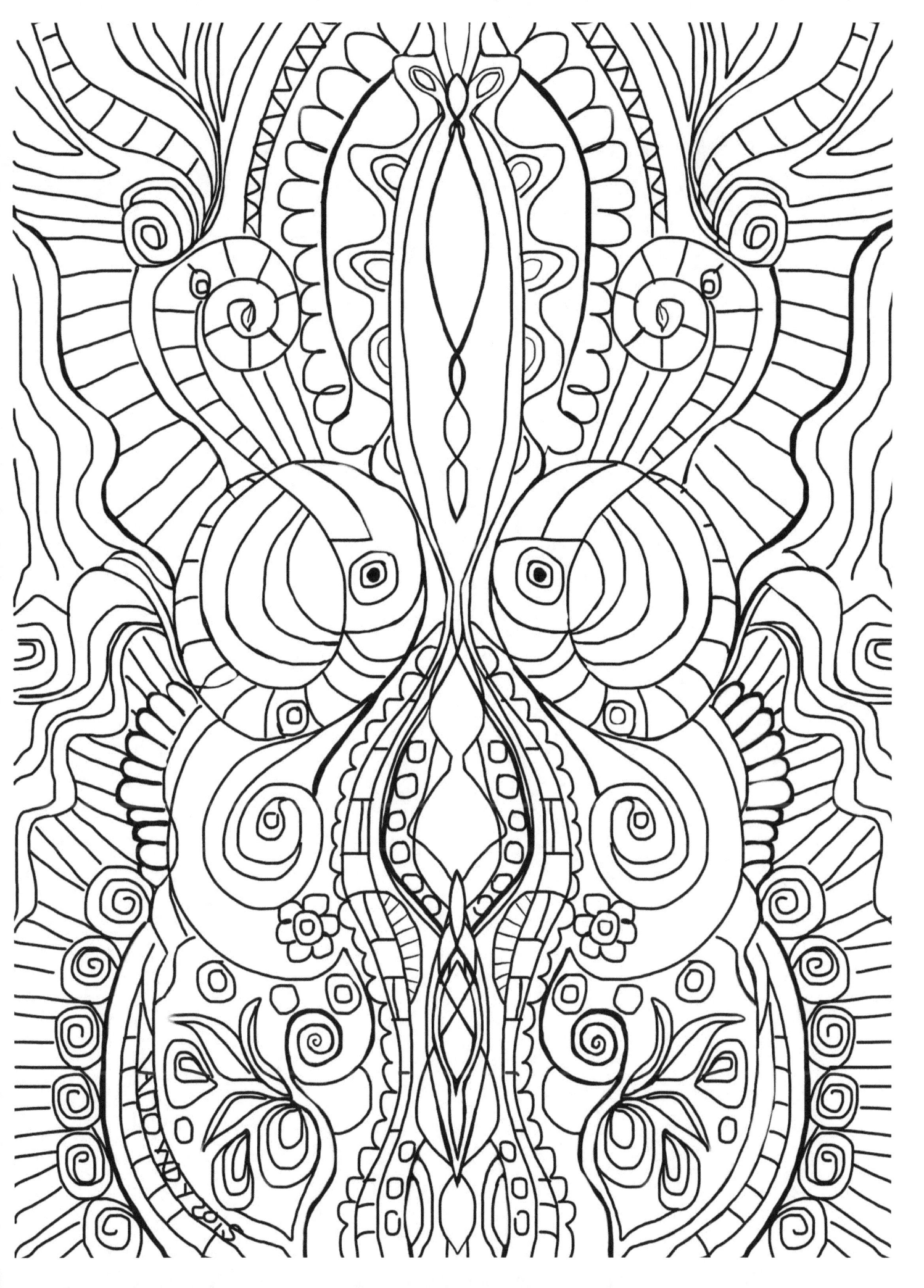

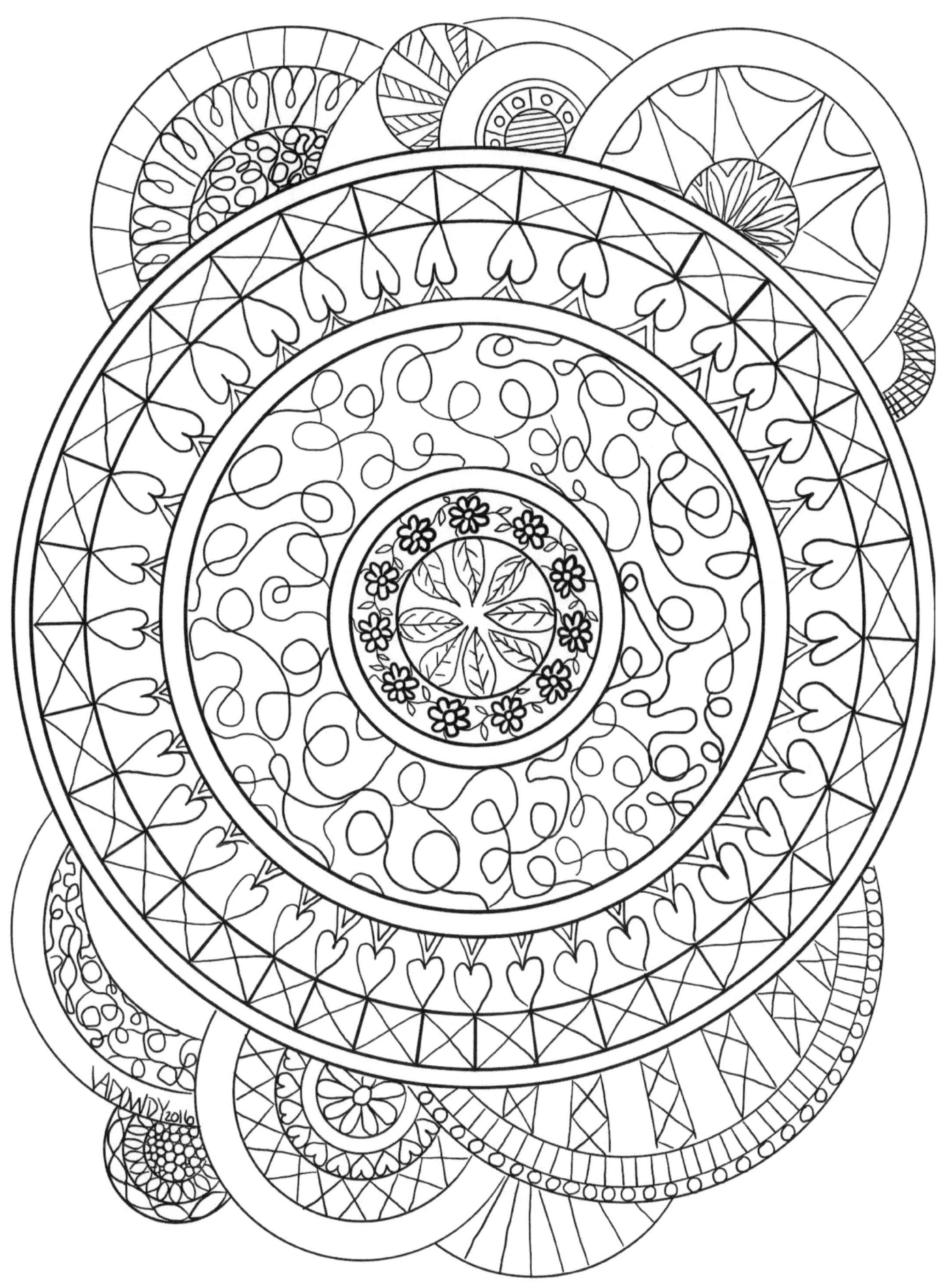

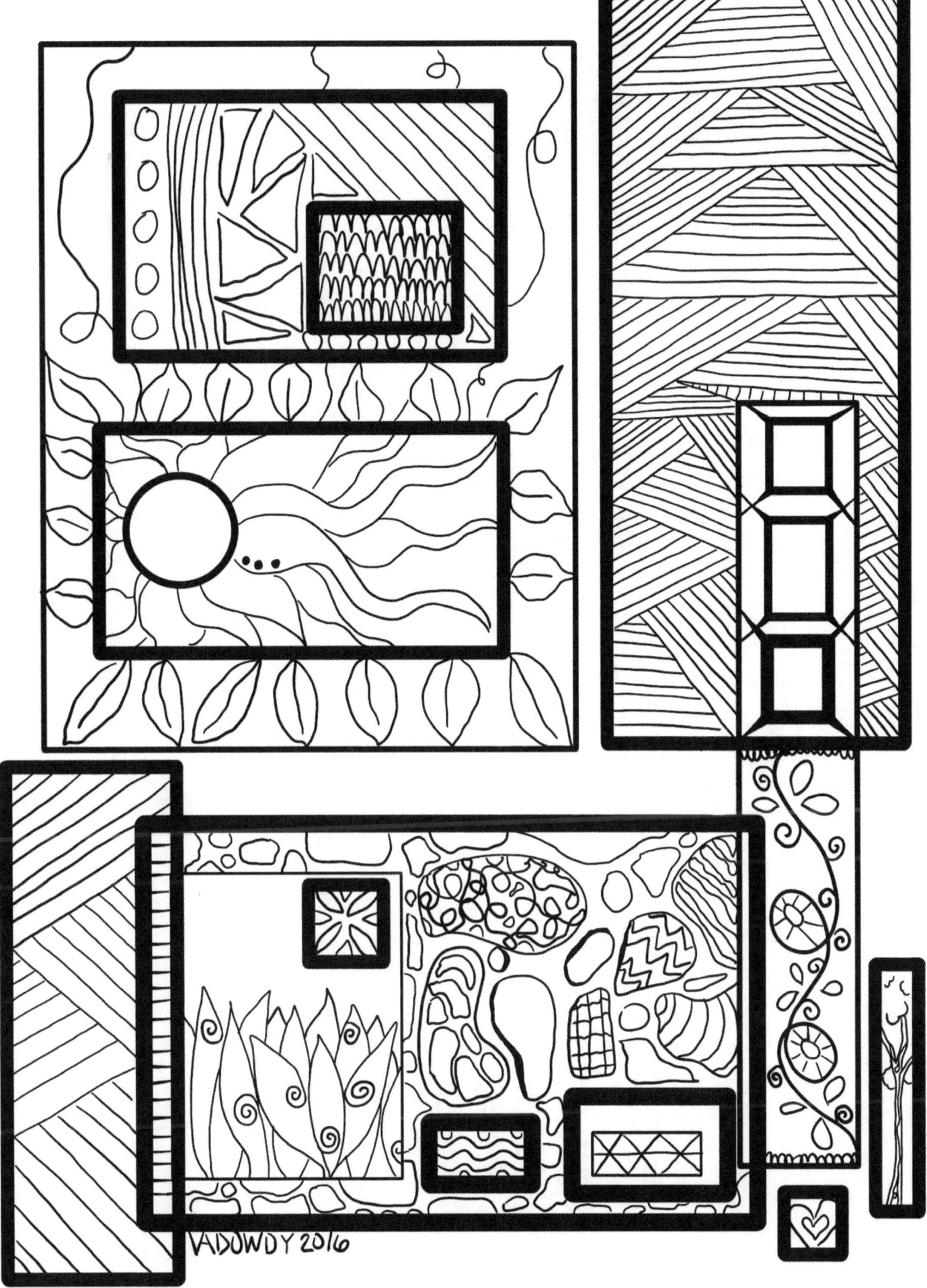

VADOWDY 2016

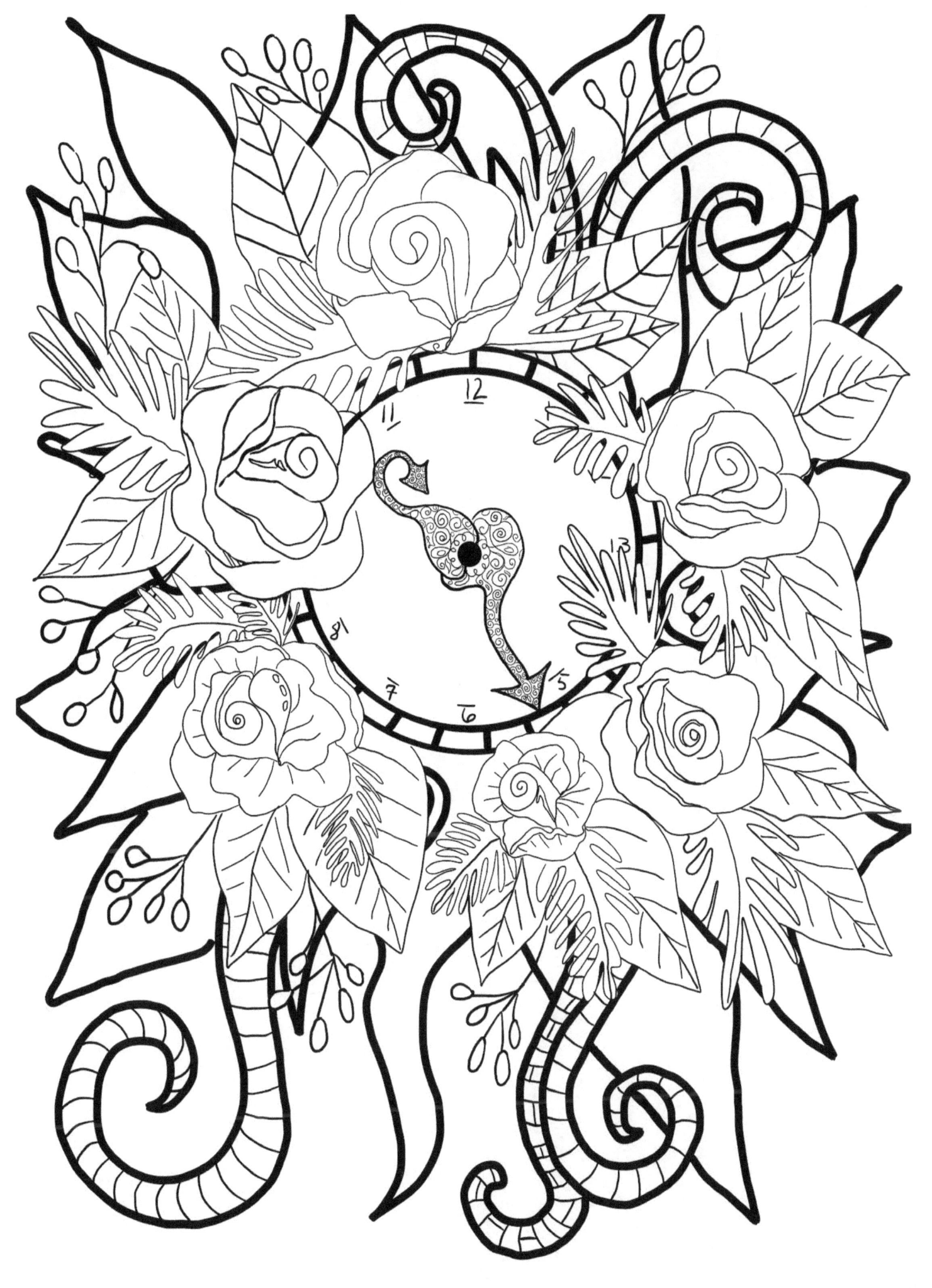

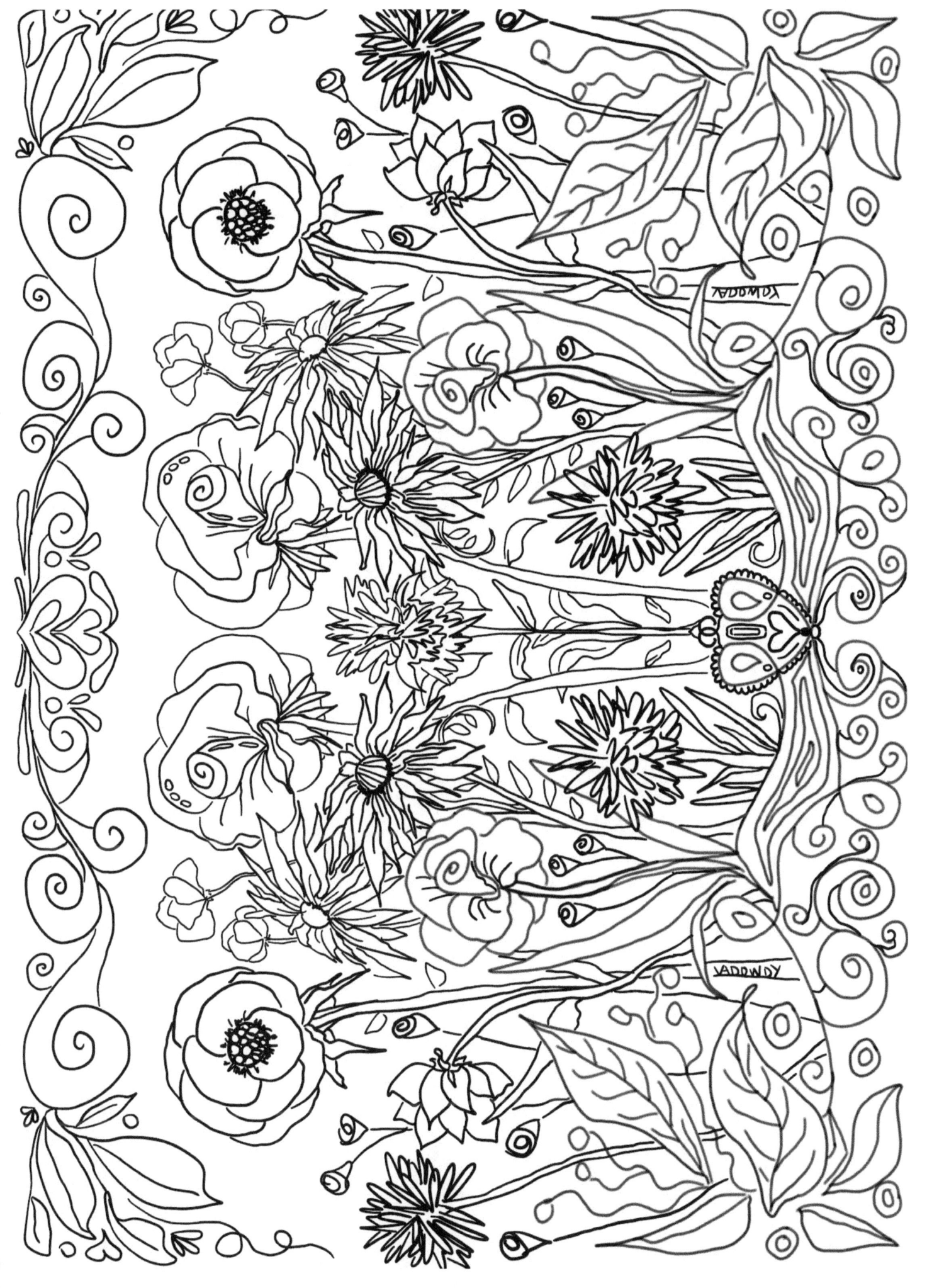

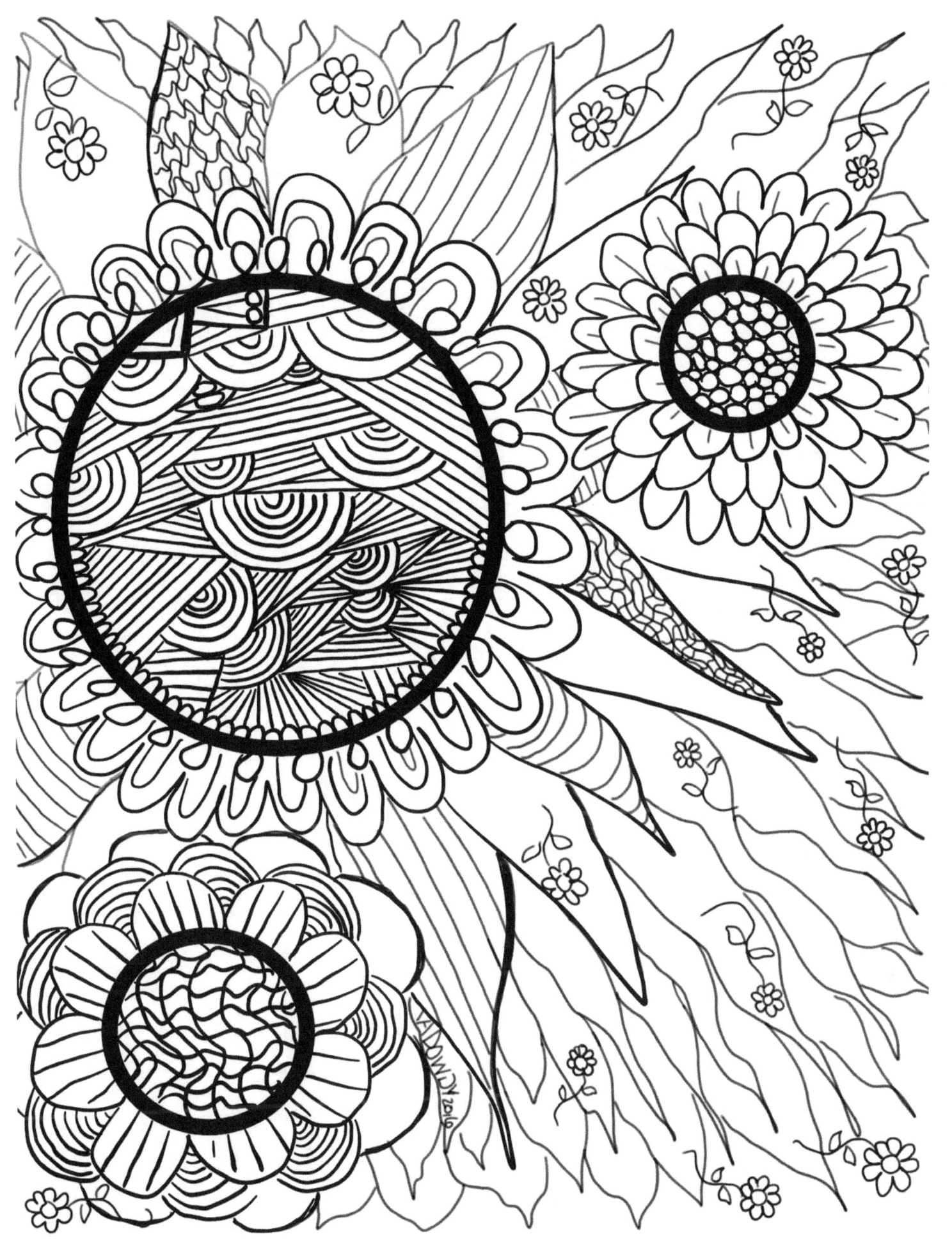

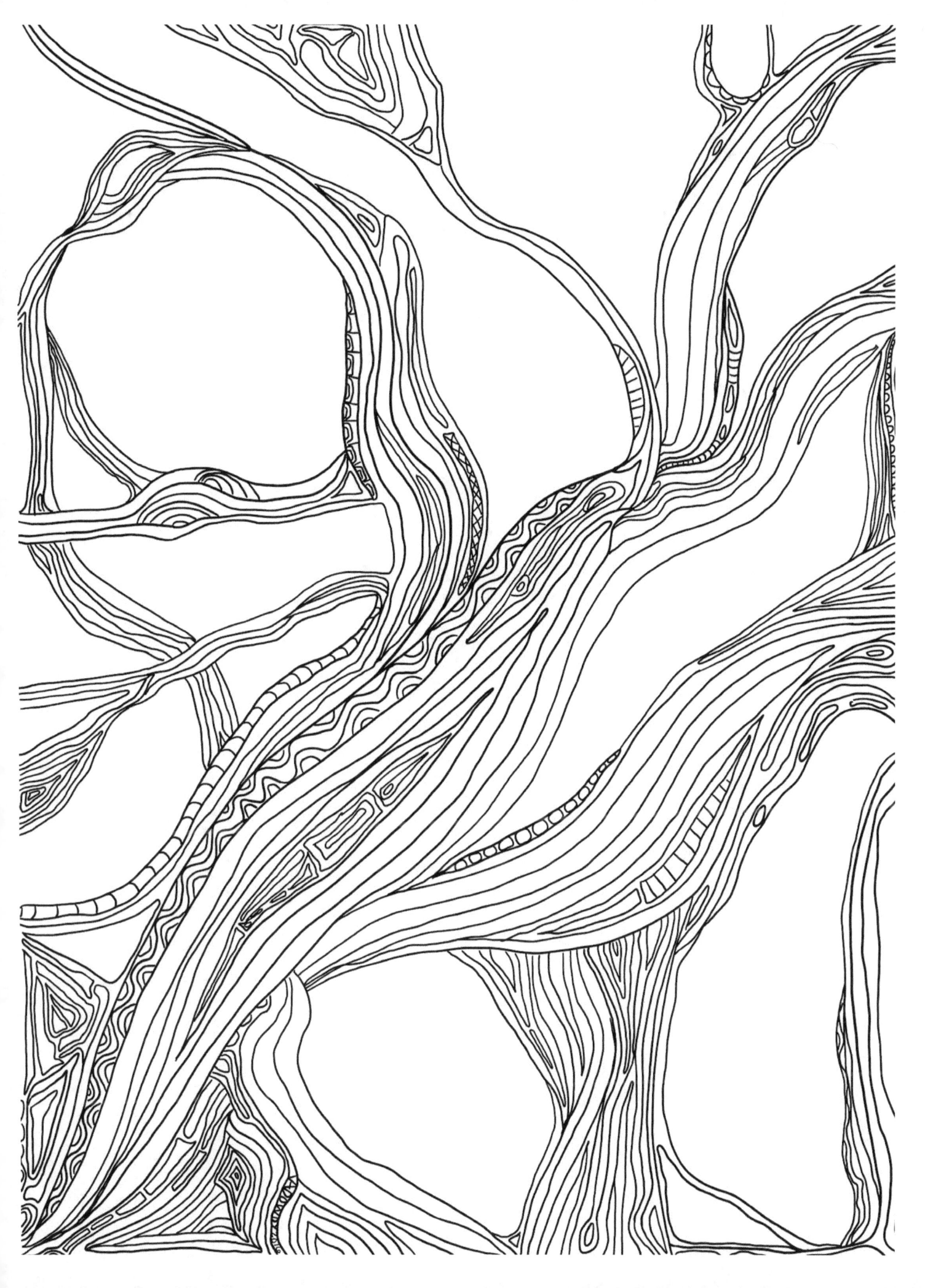

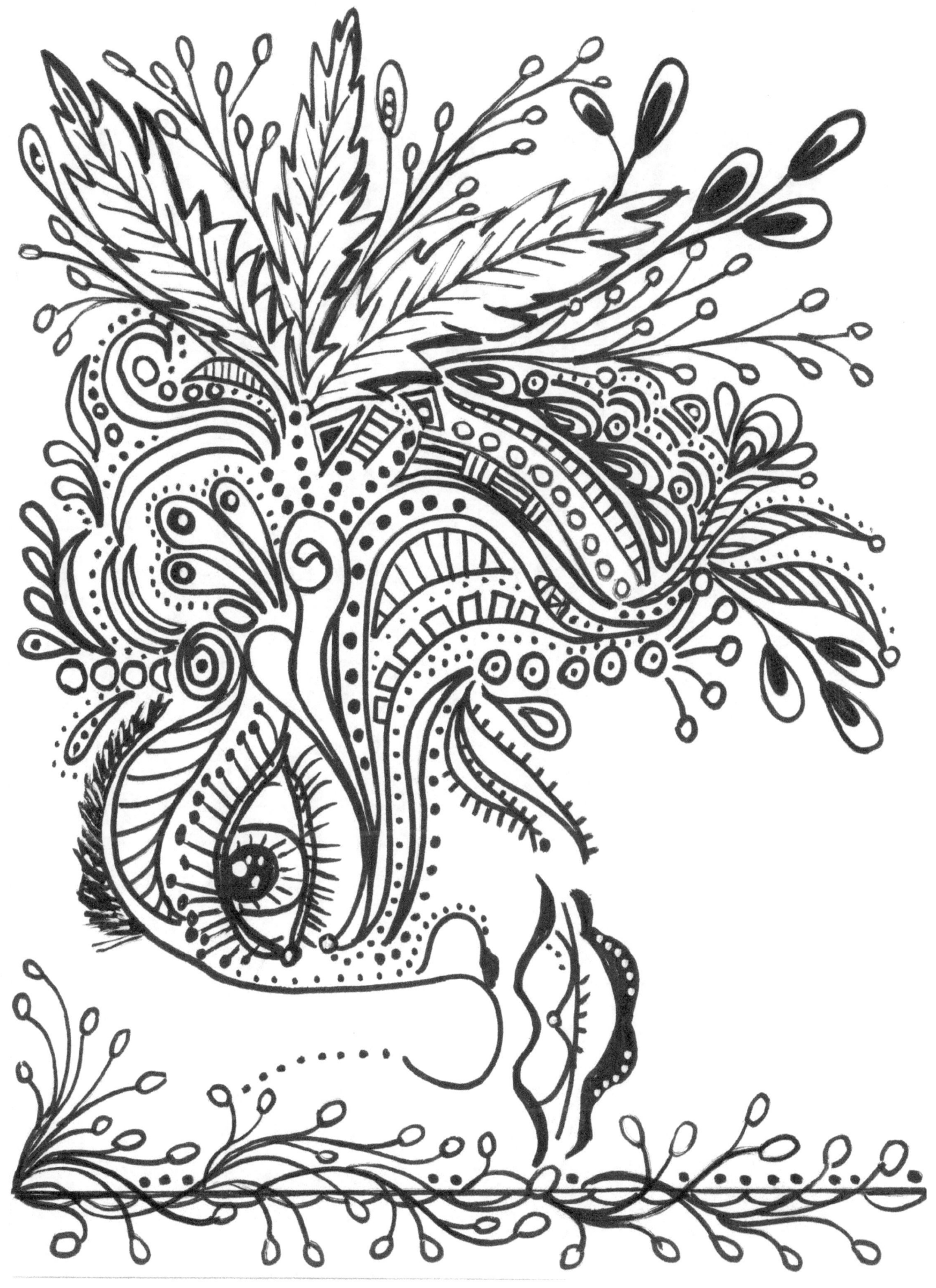

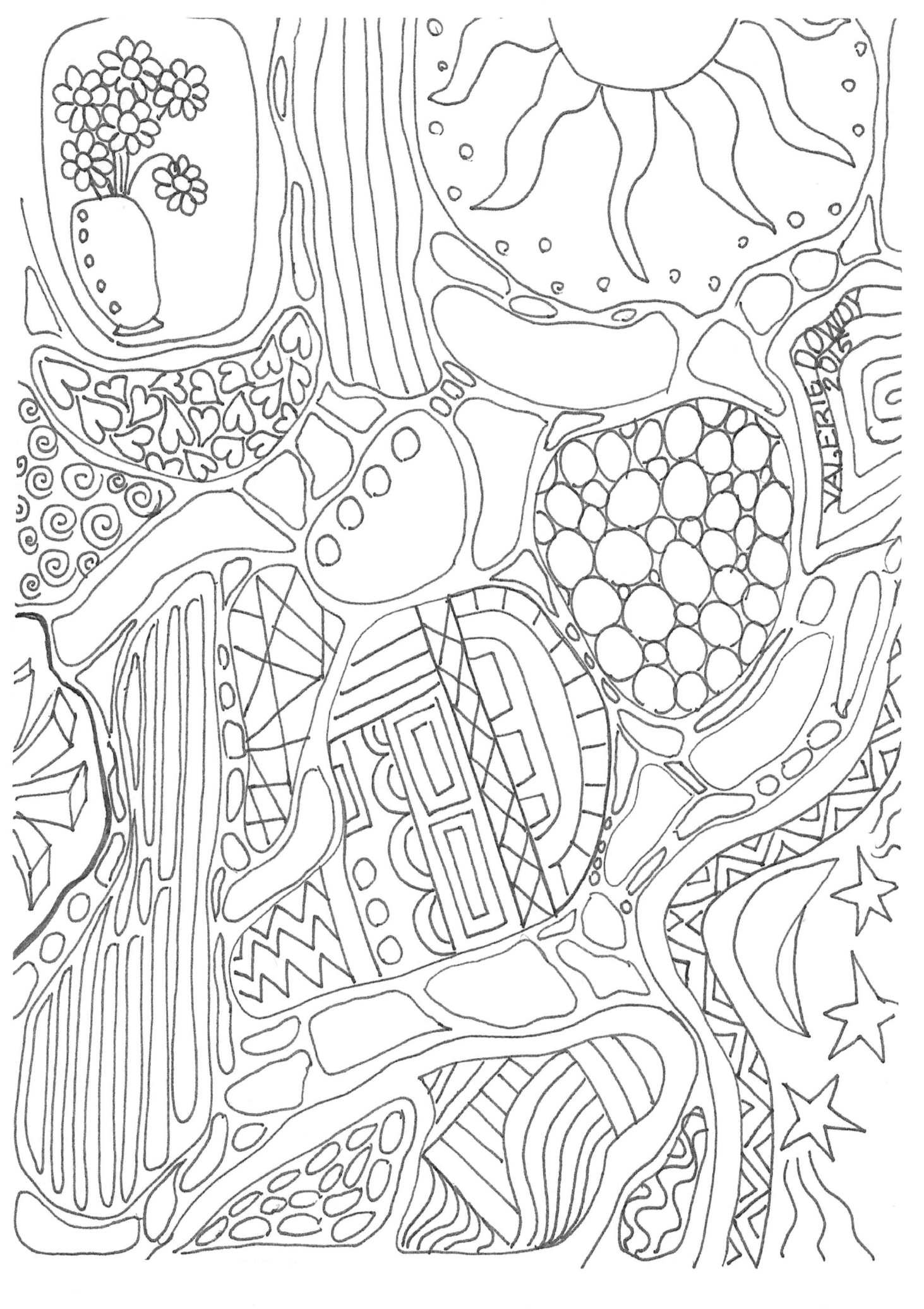

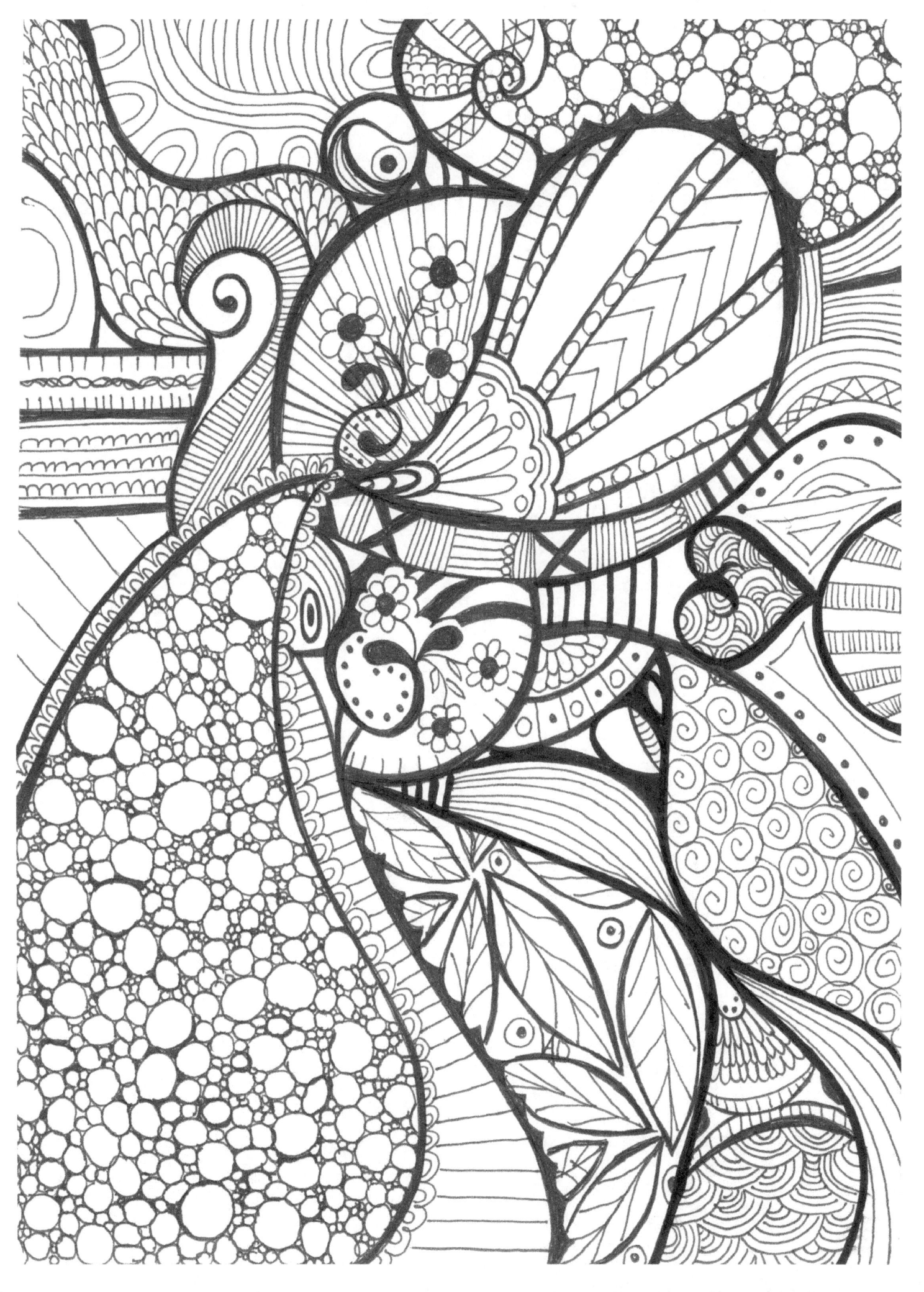

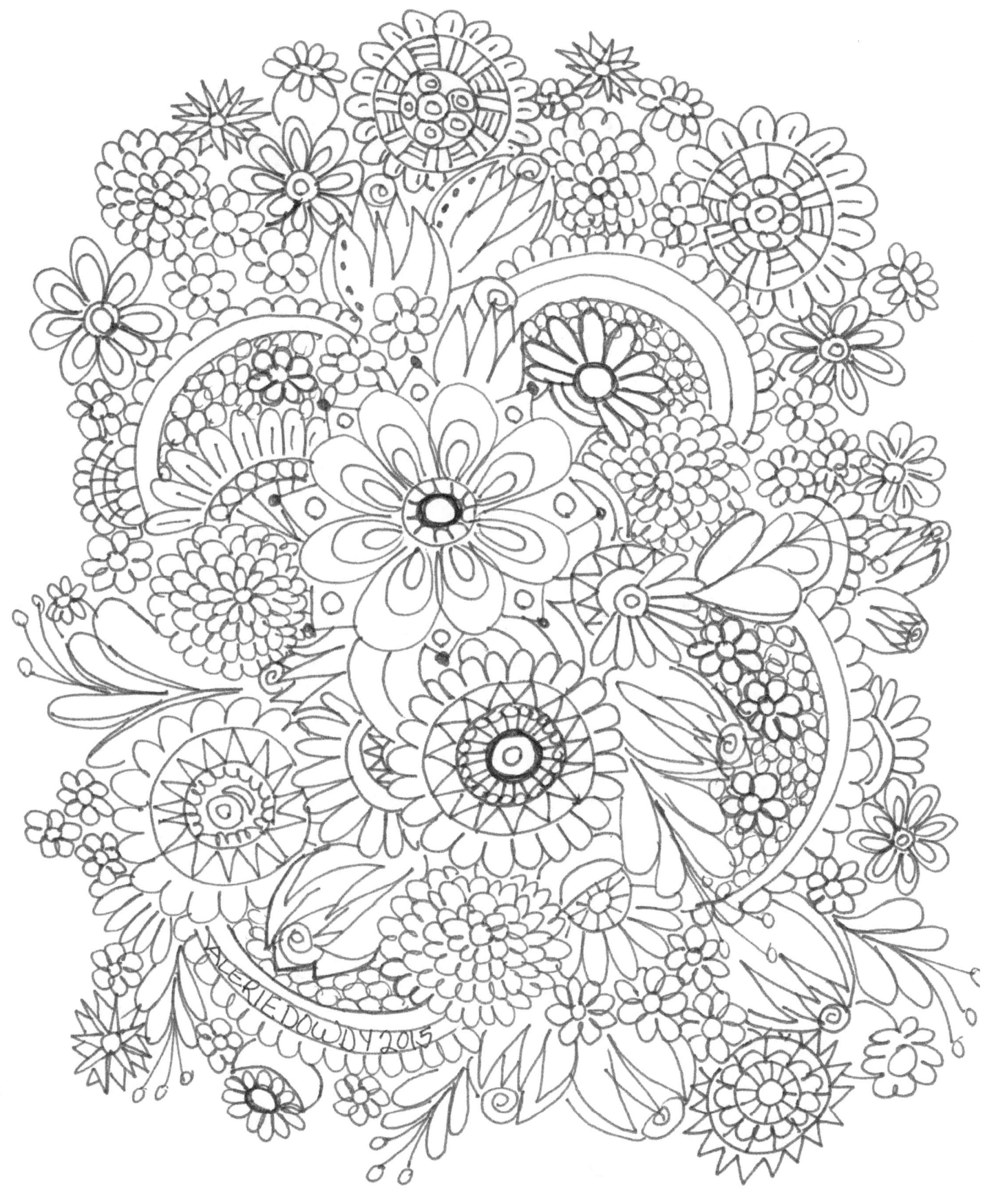

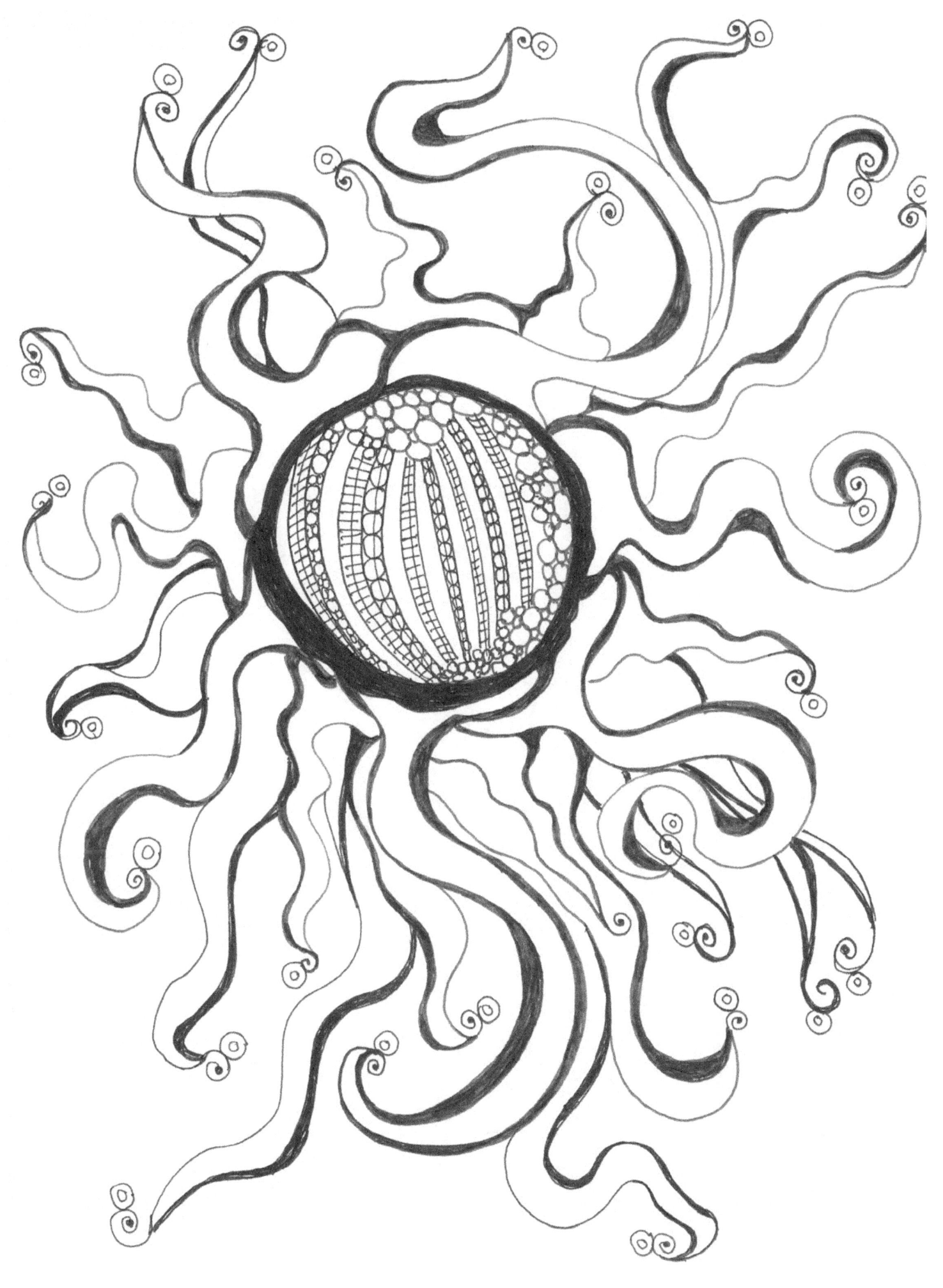

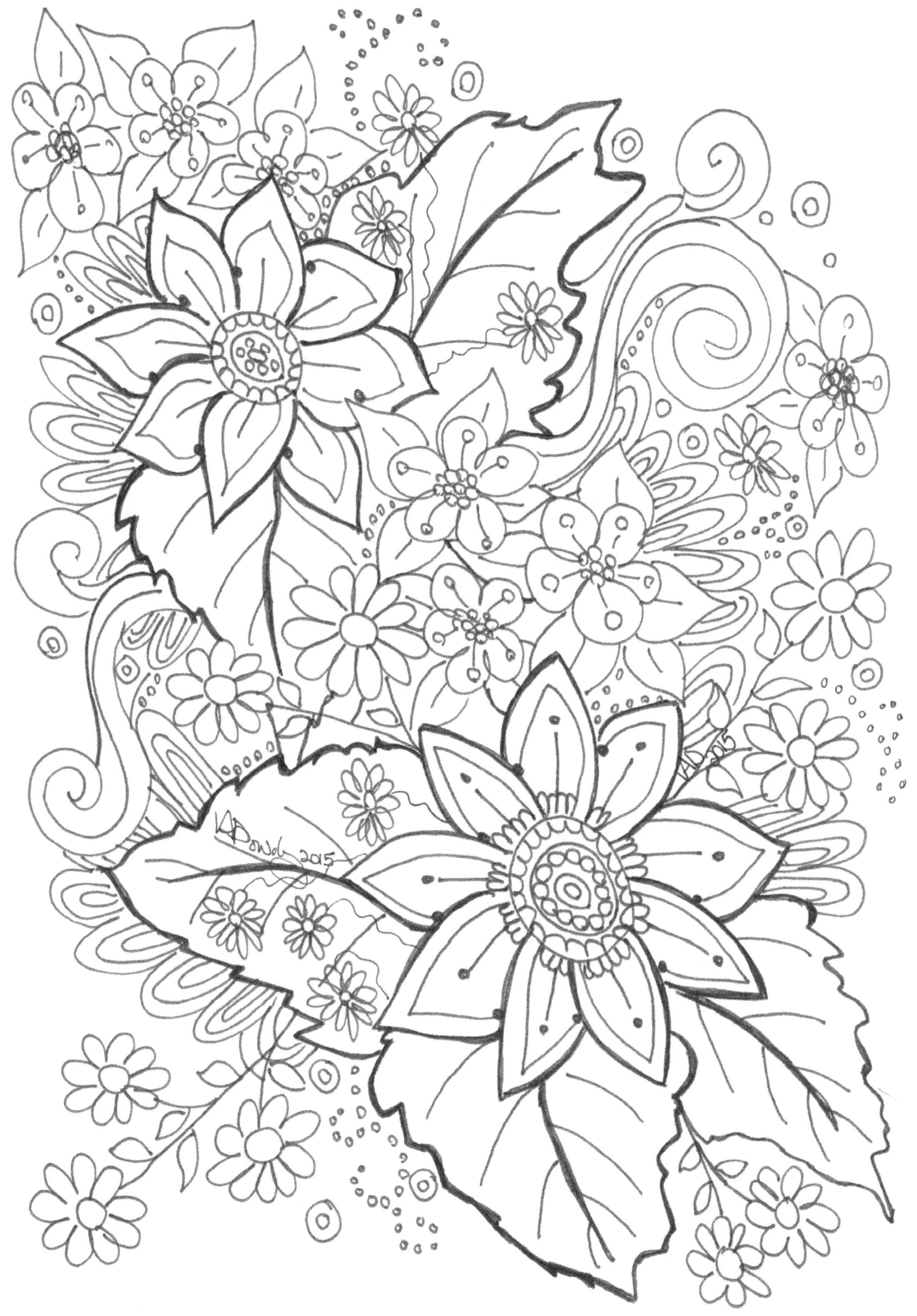

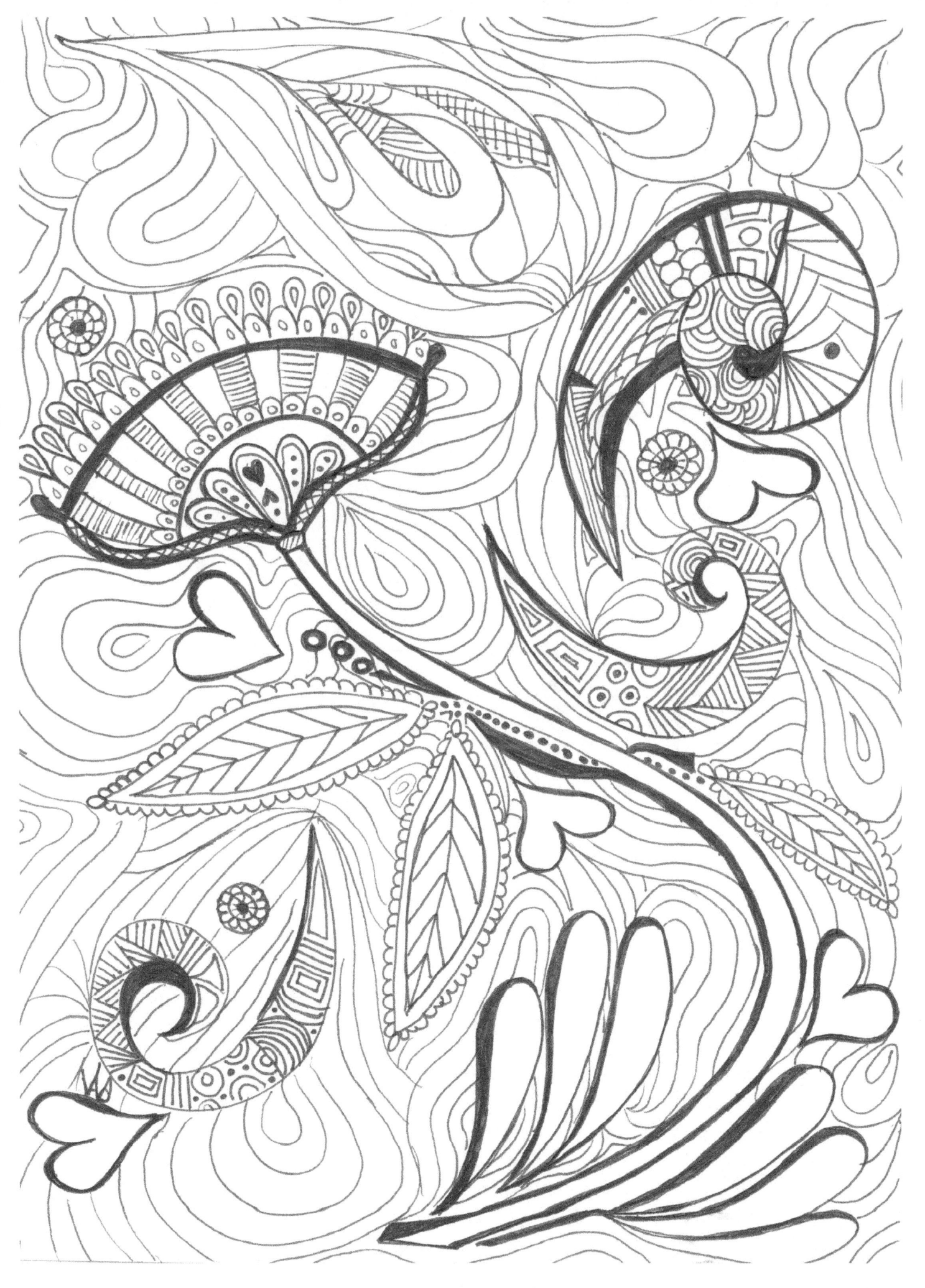

About the Author

Valerie Dowdy is a visual artist living in Southwest Virginia, where she is currently developing a series of coloring books, her art work, and a children's book (coming 2016), in which she is both author and illustrator. It is from her journals that the concept of Abstract Expressions Coloring Books were born and produced. She hopes that in sharing her work she is helping others find healing, focus and relaxation as they (re)-connect with their own creativity.

To learn more about her and her work check out her blog:
www.valeriedowdy.com

Follow Valerie on Facebook and Instagram: The Custom Brush

Contact Valerie: valerie@valeriedowdy.com